Cute Fantasy Creatures Coloring Book

Dragons, Unicorns, and Mermaids for Kids and Adults

Illustrated by Gaurav S

This book is dedicated to all the young artists and dreamers who fill the world with color and imagination. May your creativity soar as you explore the enchanting realms of fantasy.

Welcome to the Cute Fantasy Creatures Coloring Book!

Step into a magical world where dragons, unicorns, and mermaids come to life with every stroke of your pencil. This book is designed for both children and adults who love to color and explore their creativity. Inside, you'll find over 50 beautifully illustrated pages, each featuring a unique and whimsical scene ready for you to bring to life with color.

What's Inside:

- Dragons: Friendly and playful dragons in medieval landscapes, castles, and treasure-filled caves.
- Unicorns: Majestic unicorns in enchanted forests, under rainbows, and on fluffy clouds.
- Mermaids: Graceful mermaids swimming in vibrant underwater worlds, surrounded by coral reefs and sea creatures.

Each page is single-sided to prevent bleed-through, making it perfect for crayons, colored pencils, markers, or gel pens. Whether you're looking to relax, unwind, or simply enjoy the art of coloring, this book offers something for everyone.

Grab your favorite coloring tools and embark on a fantastical journey filled with fun, relaxation, and endless creativity. Let your imagination run wild!

Happy Coloring!

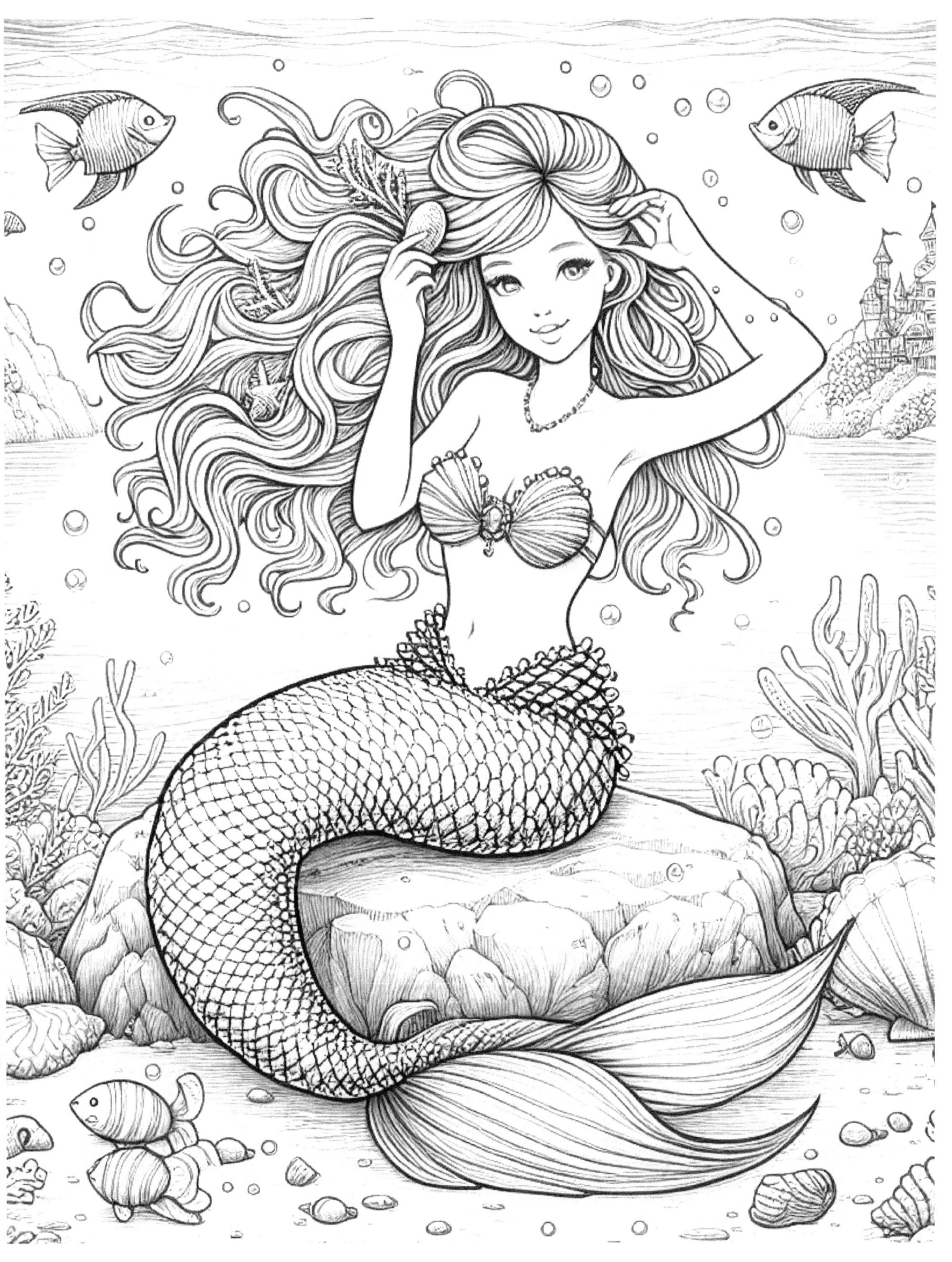

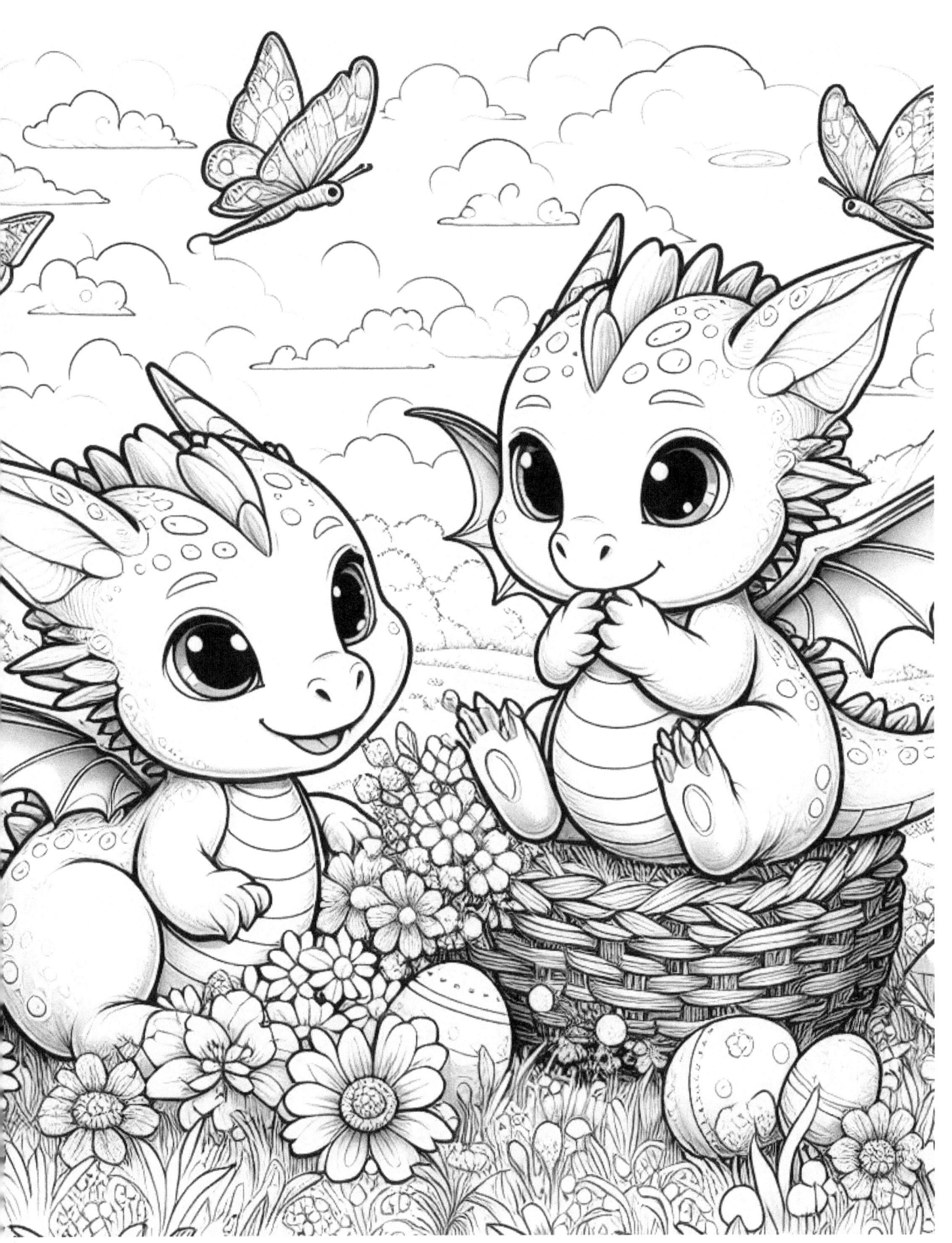

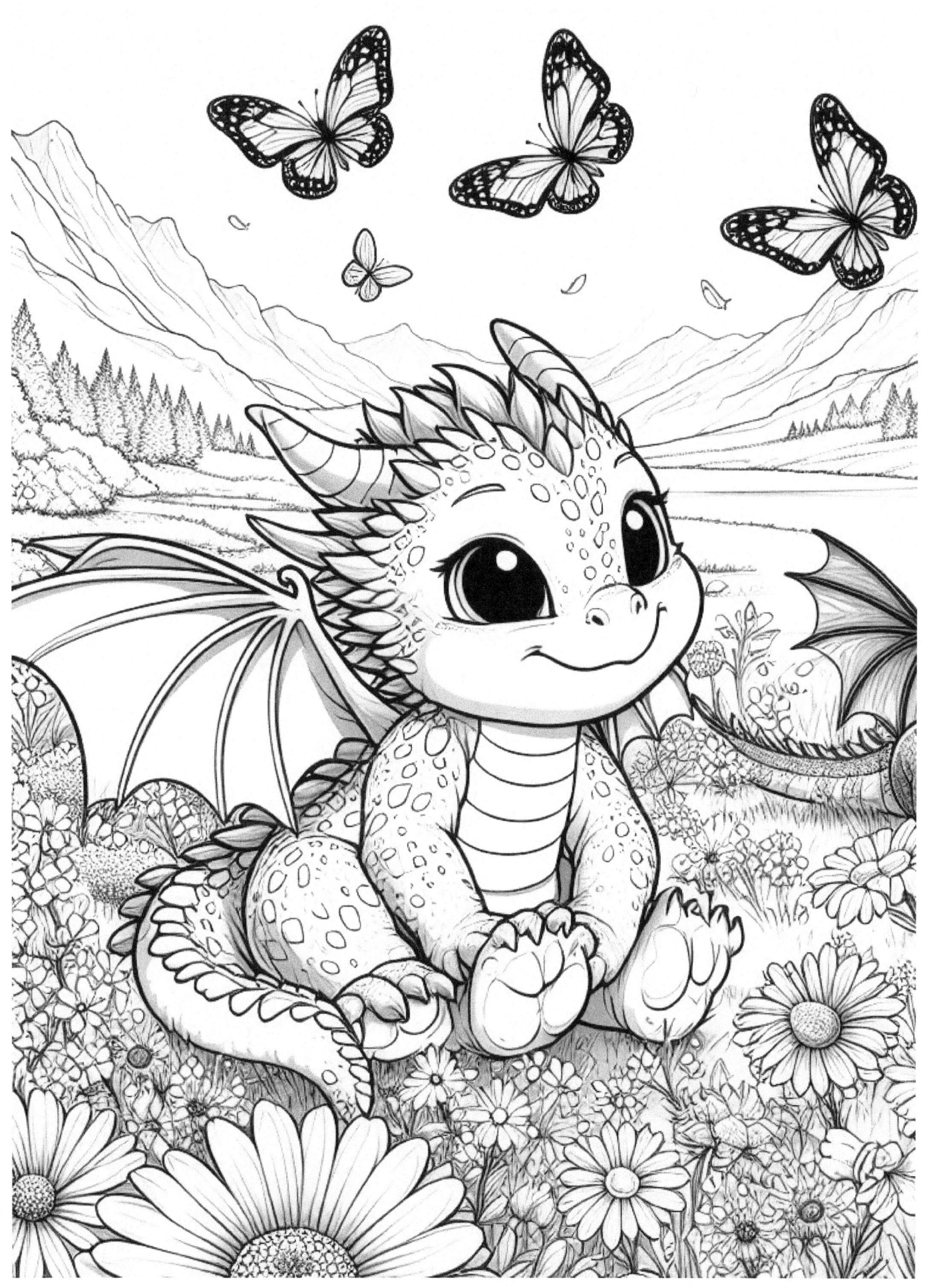

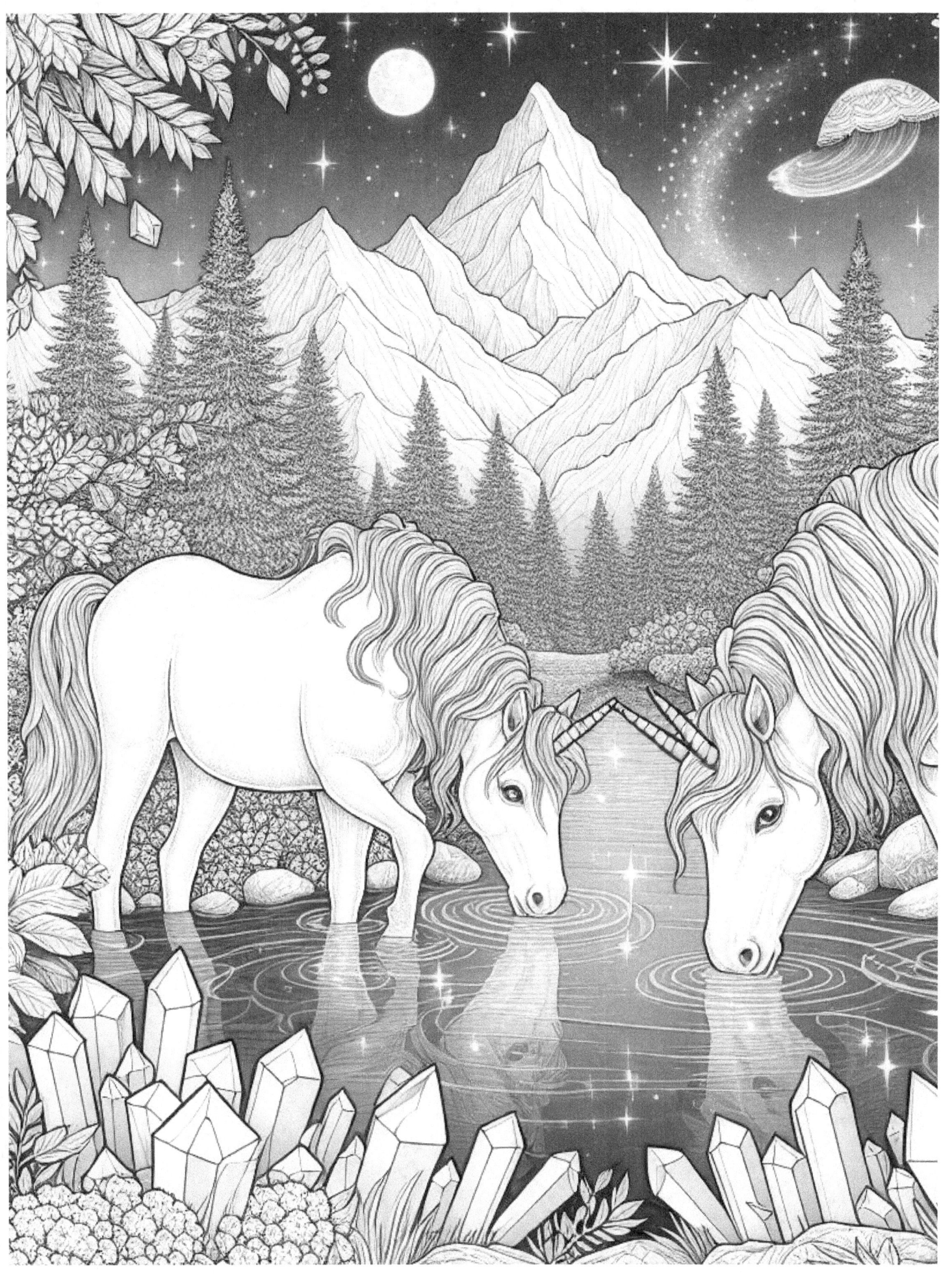

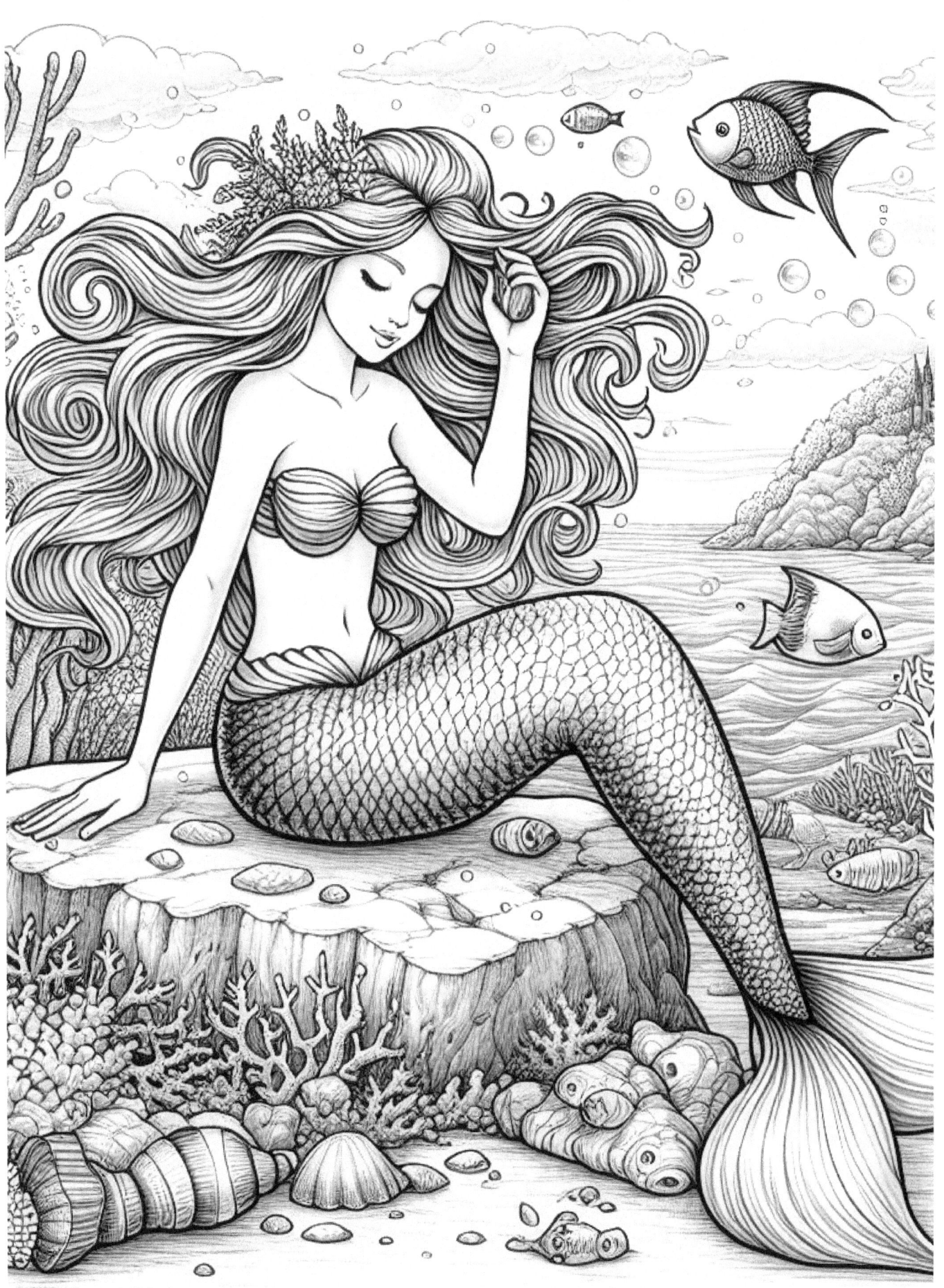

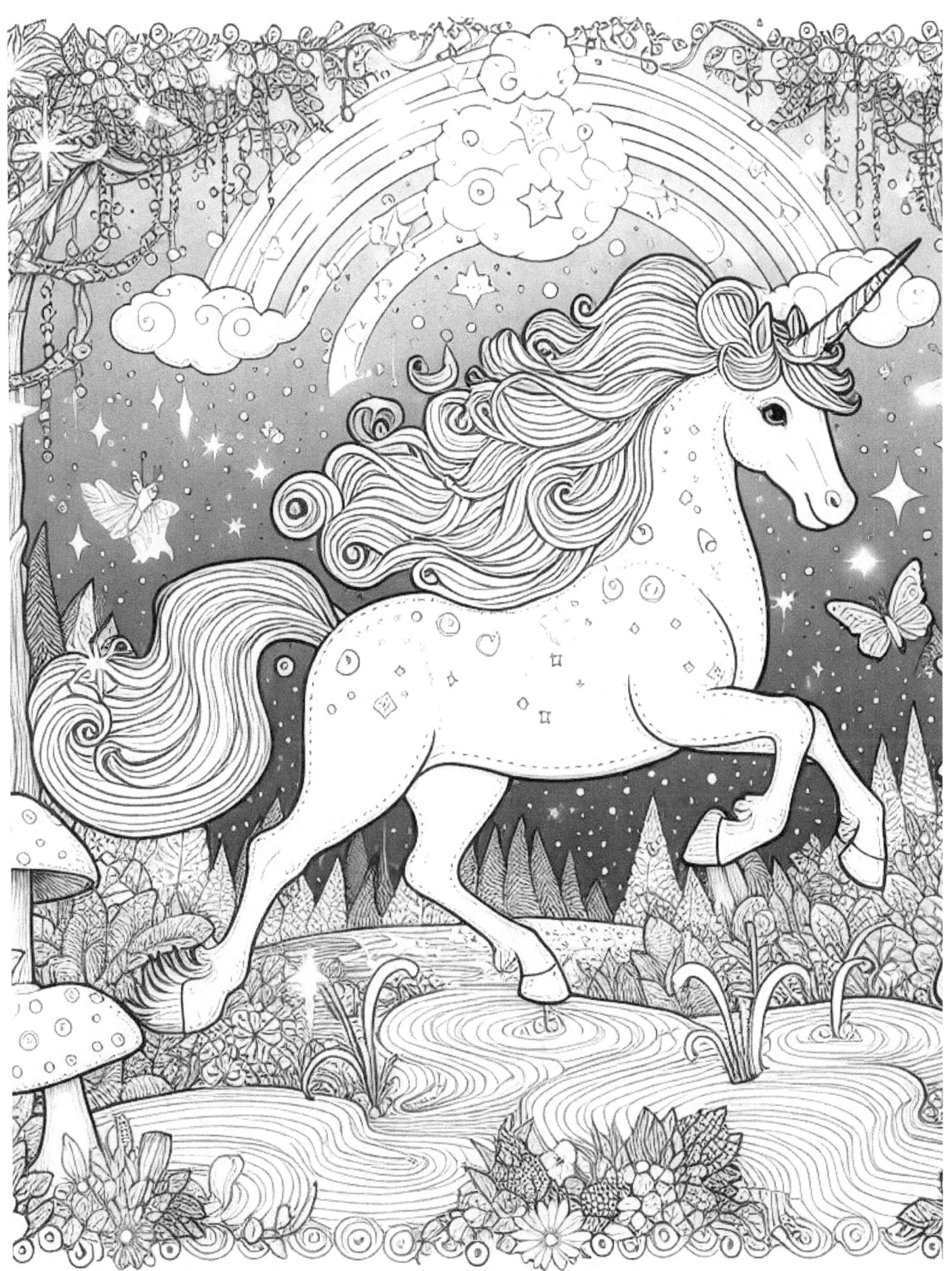

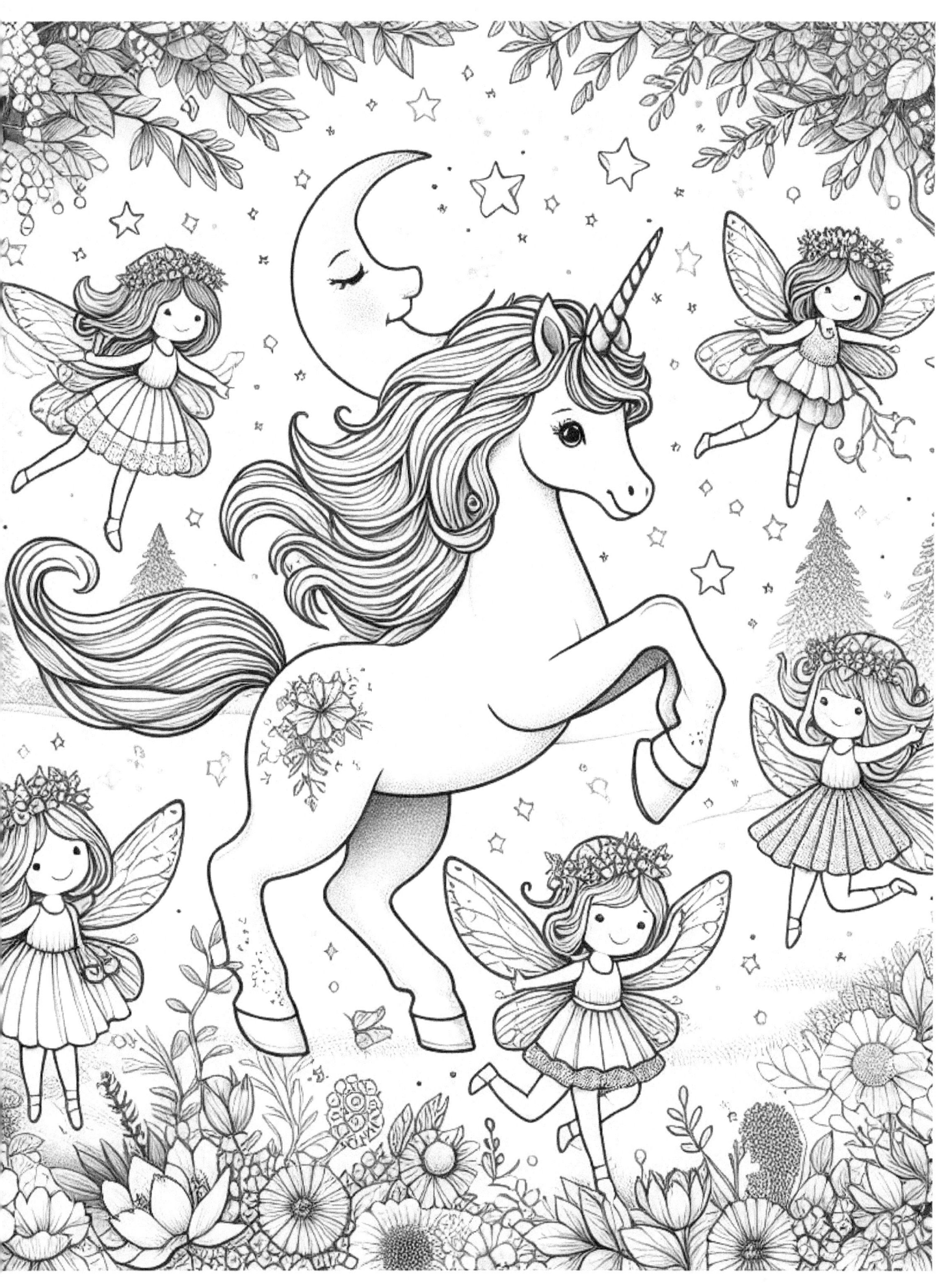

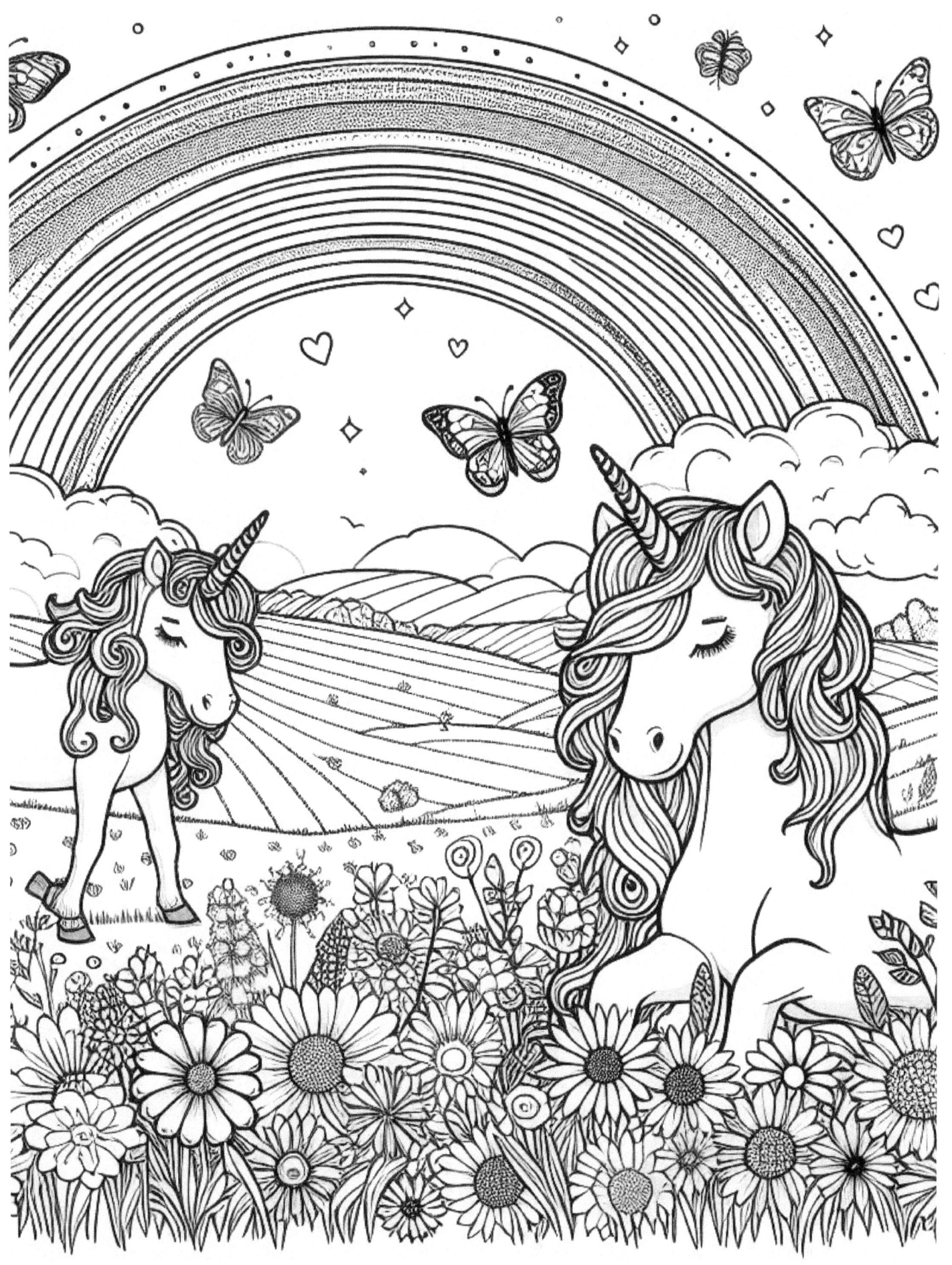

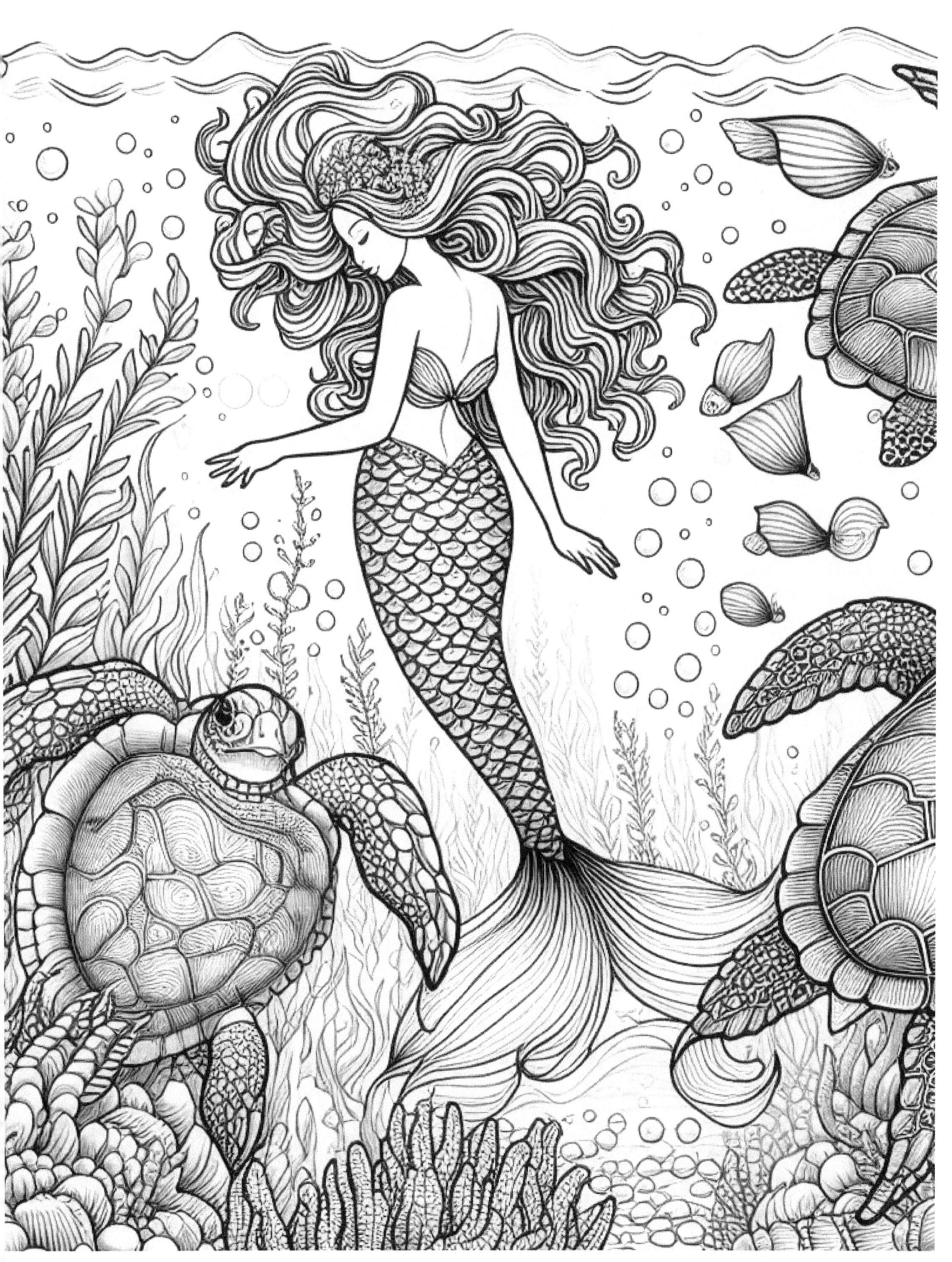

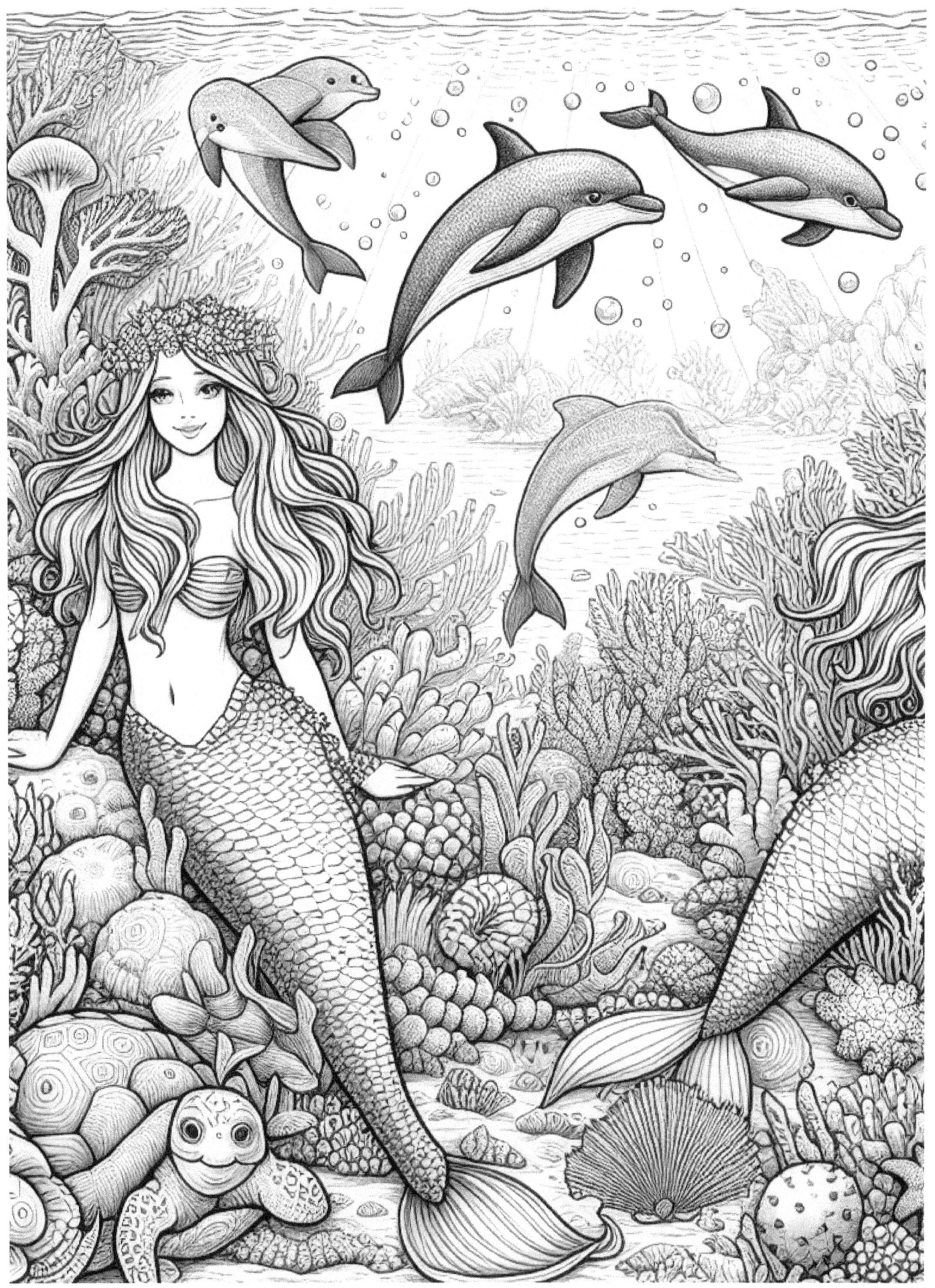

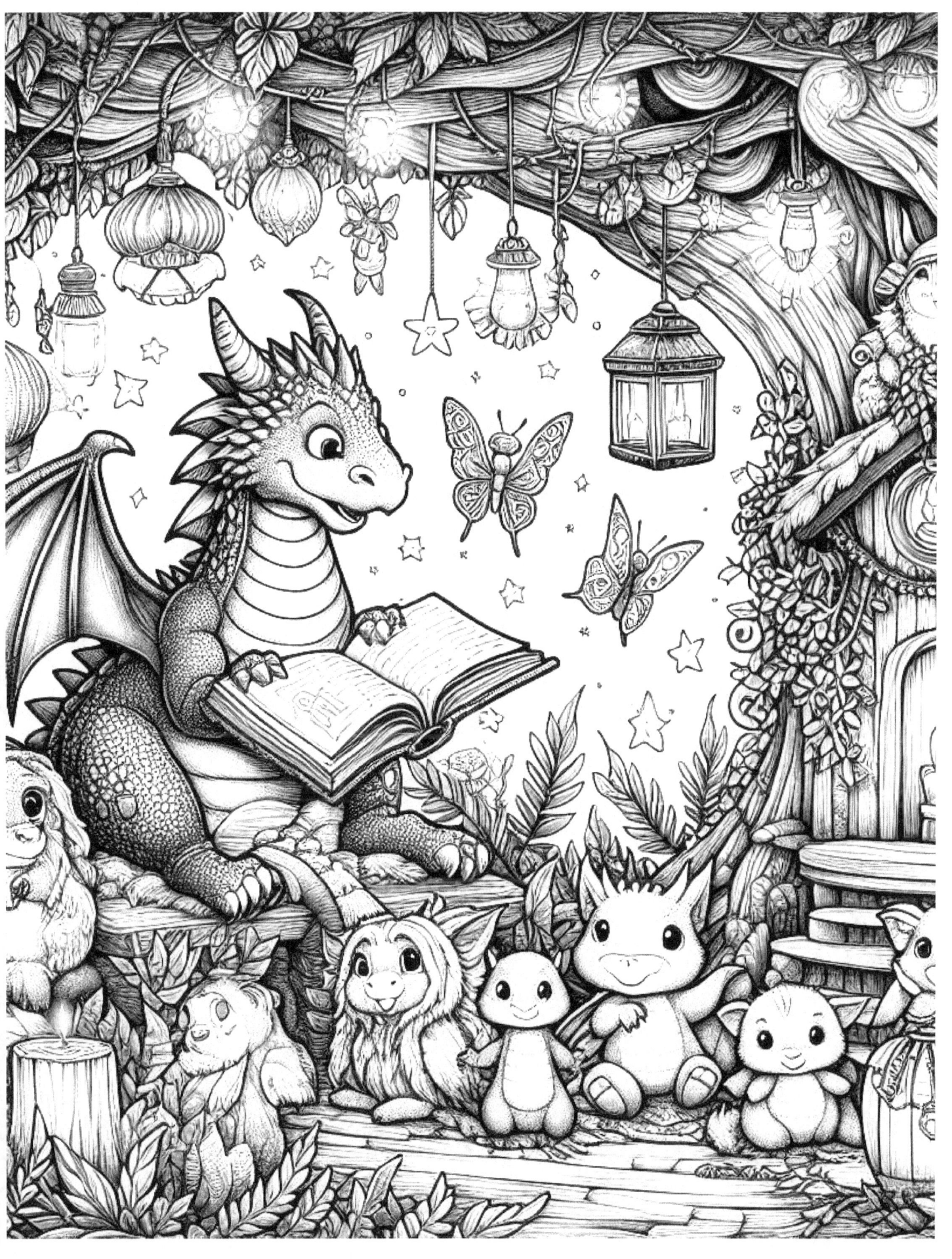

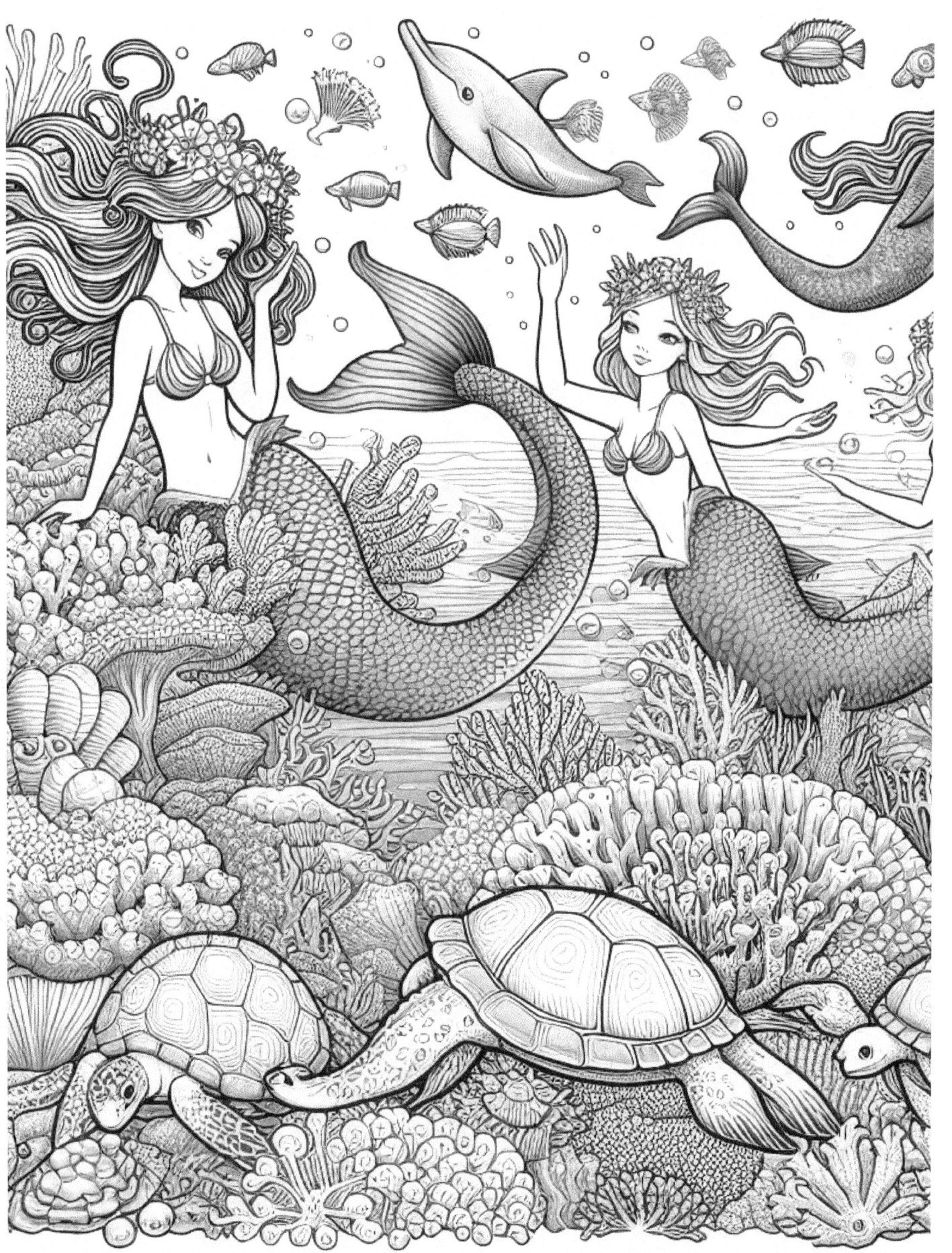

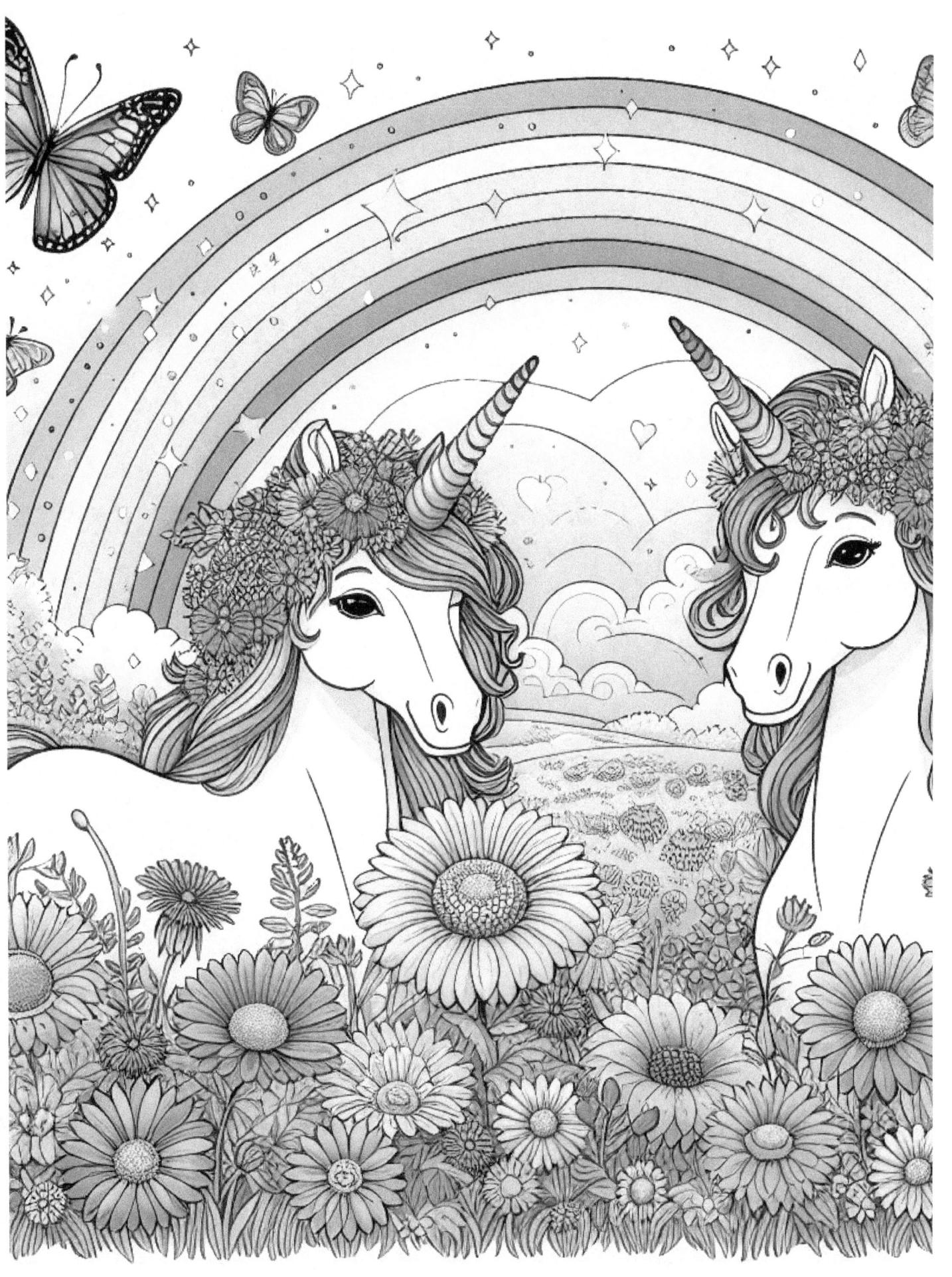

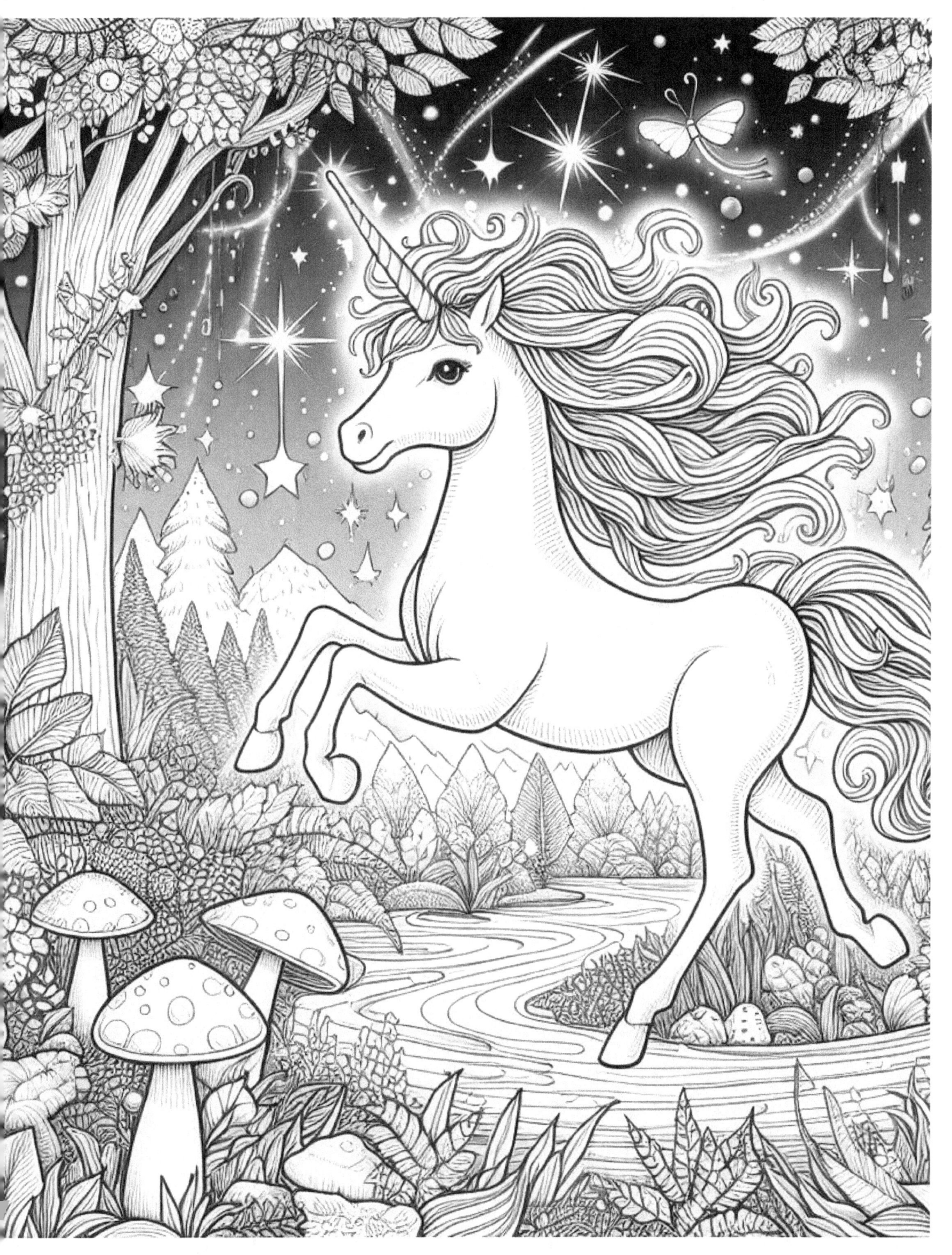

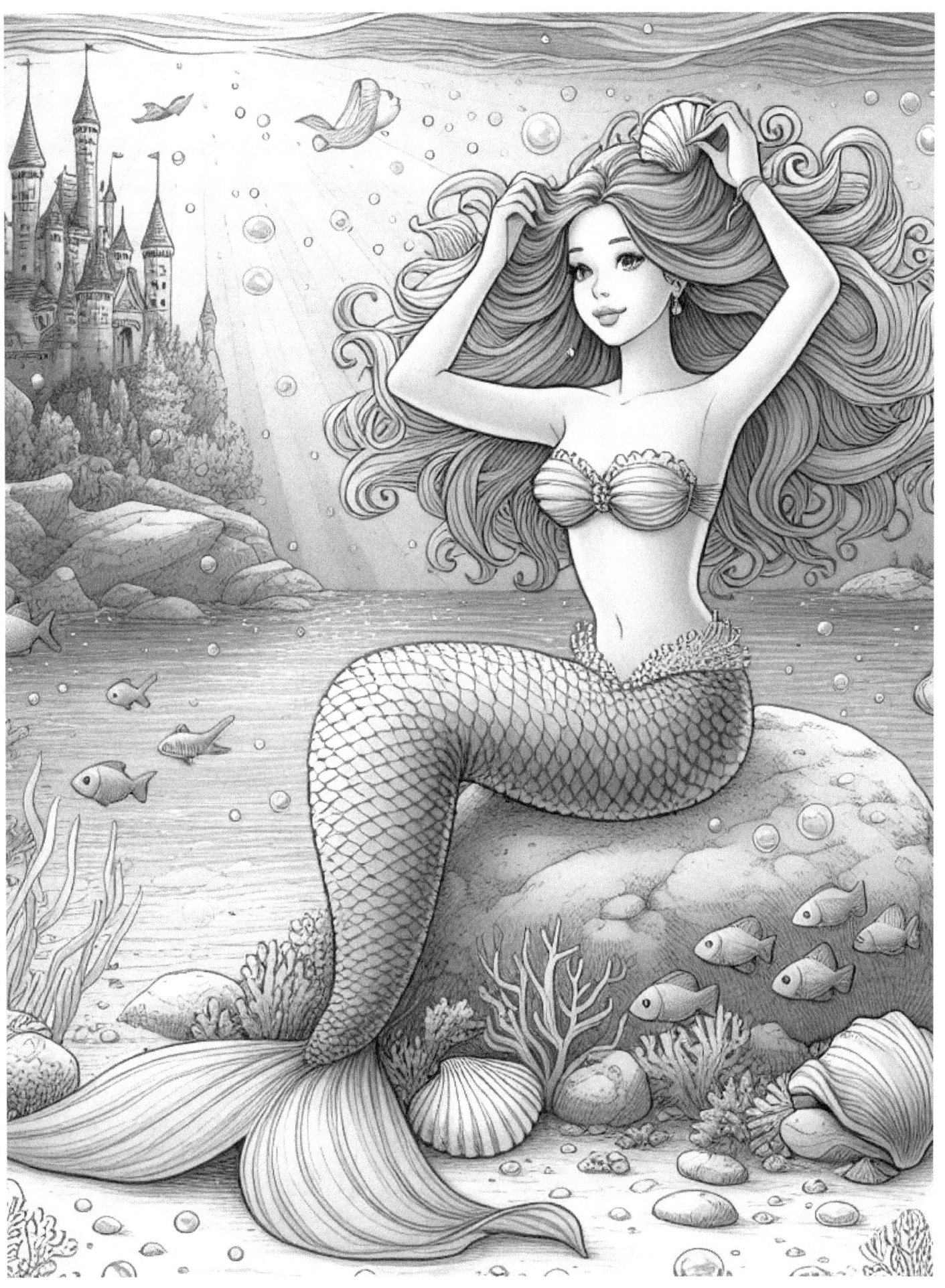

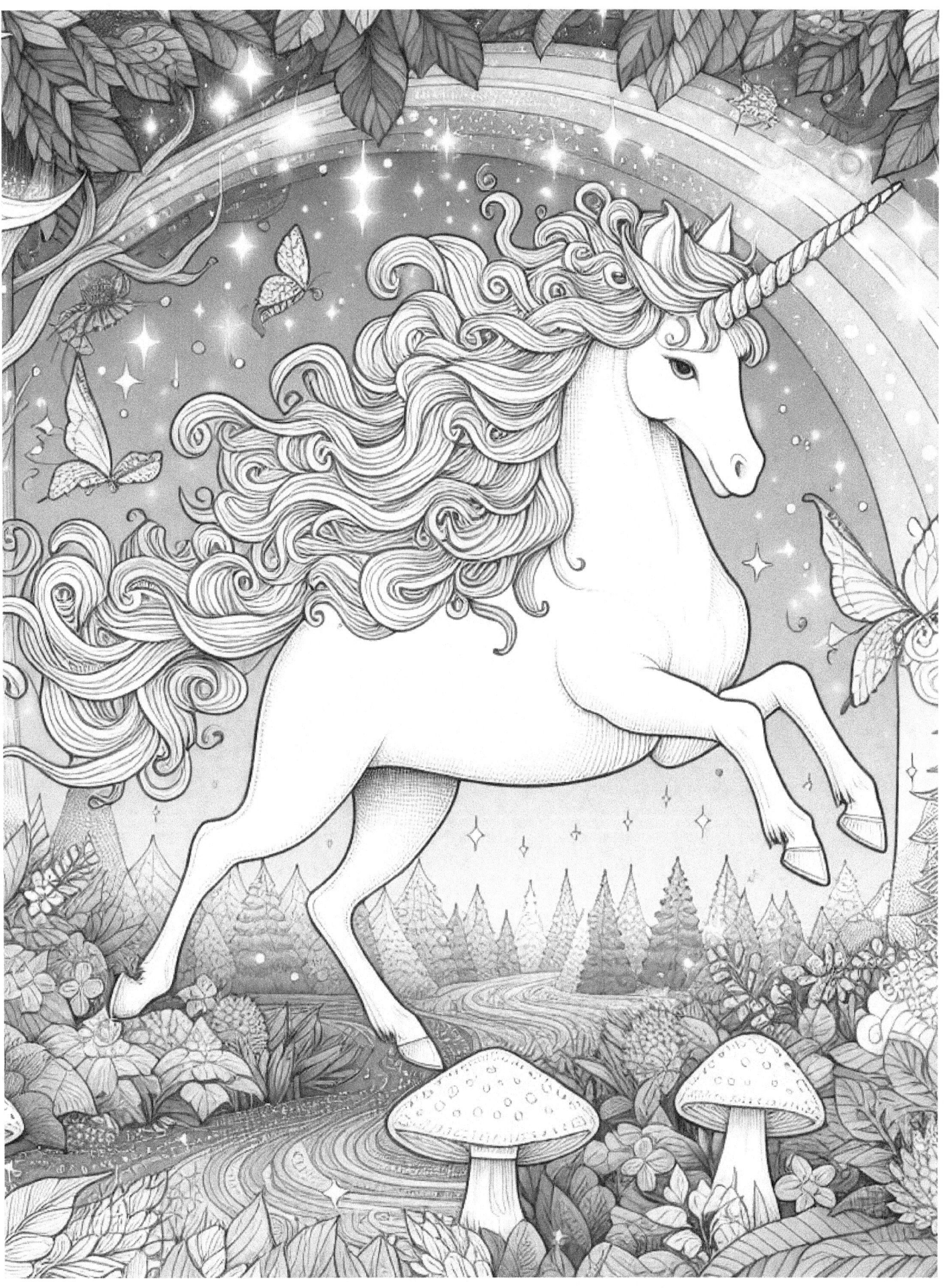

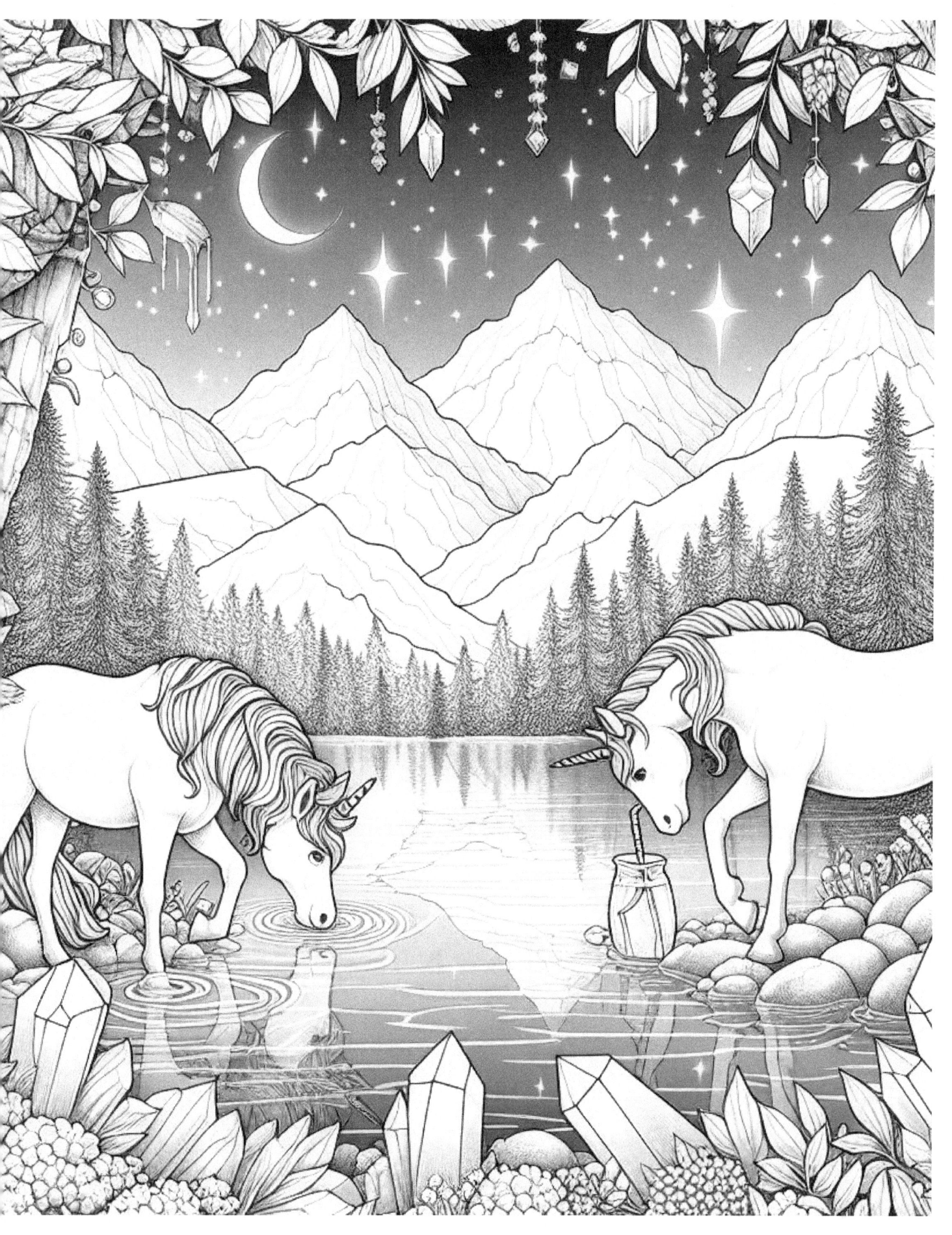

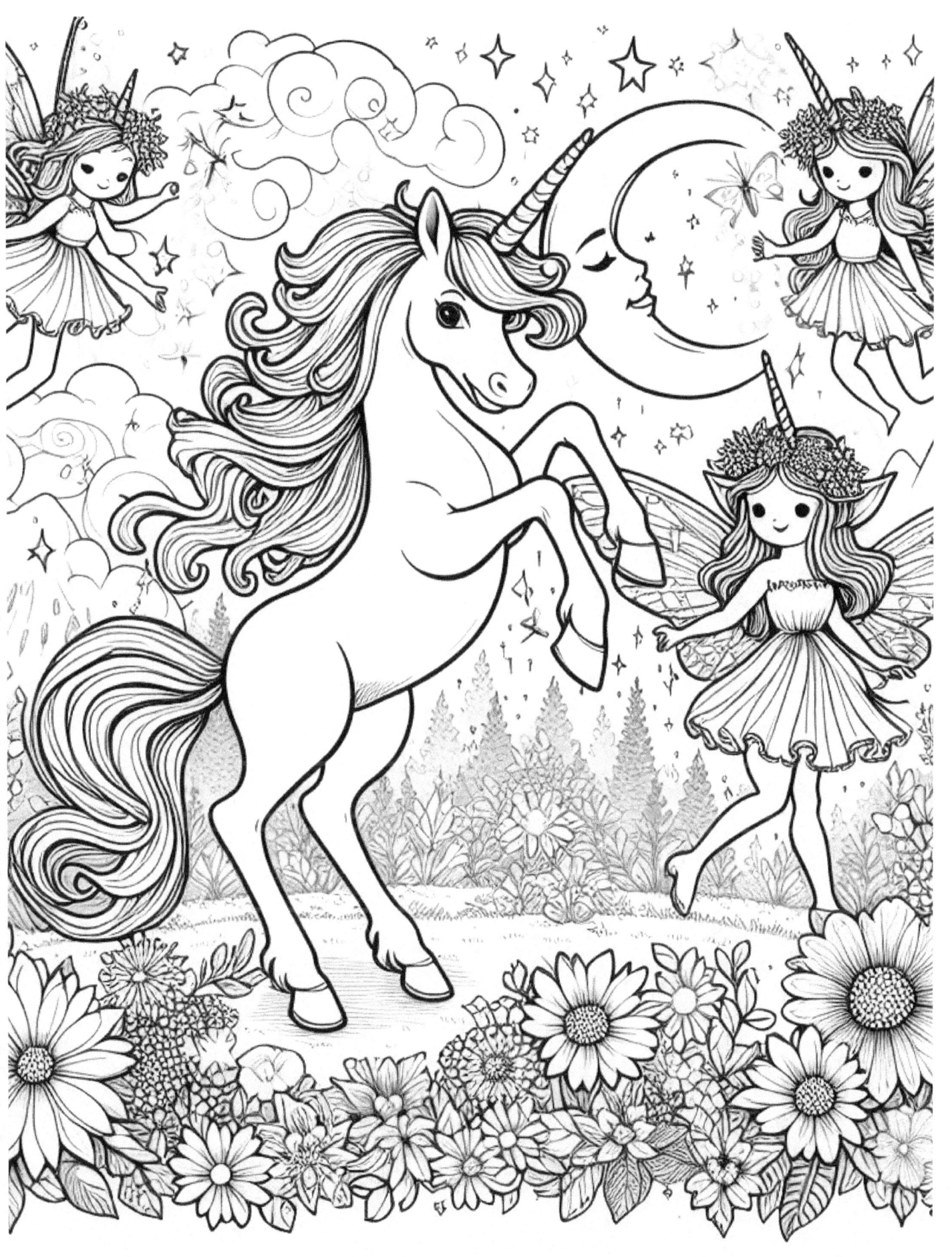

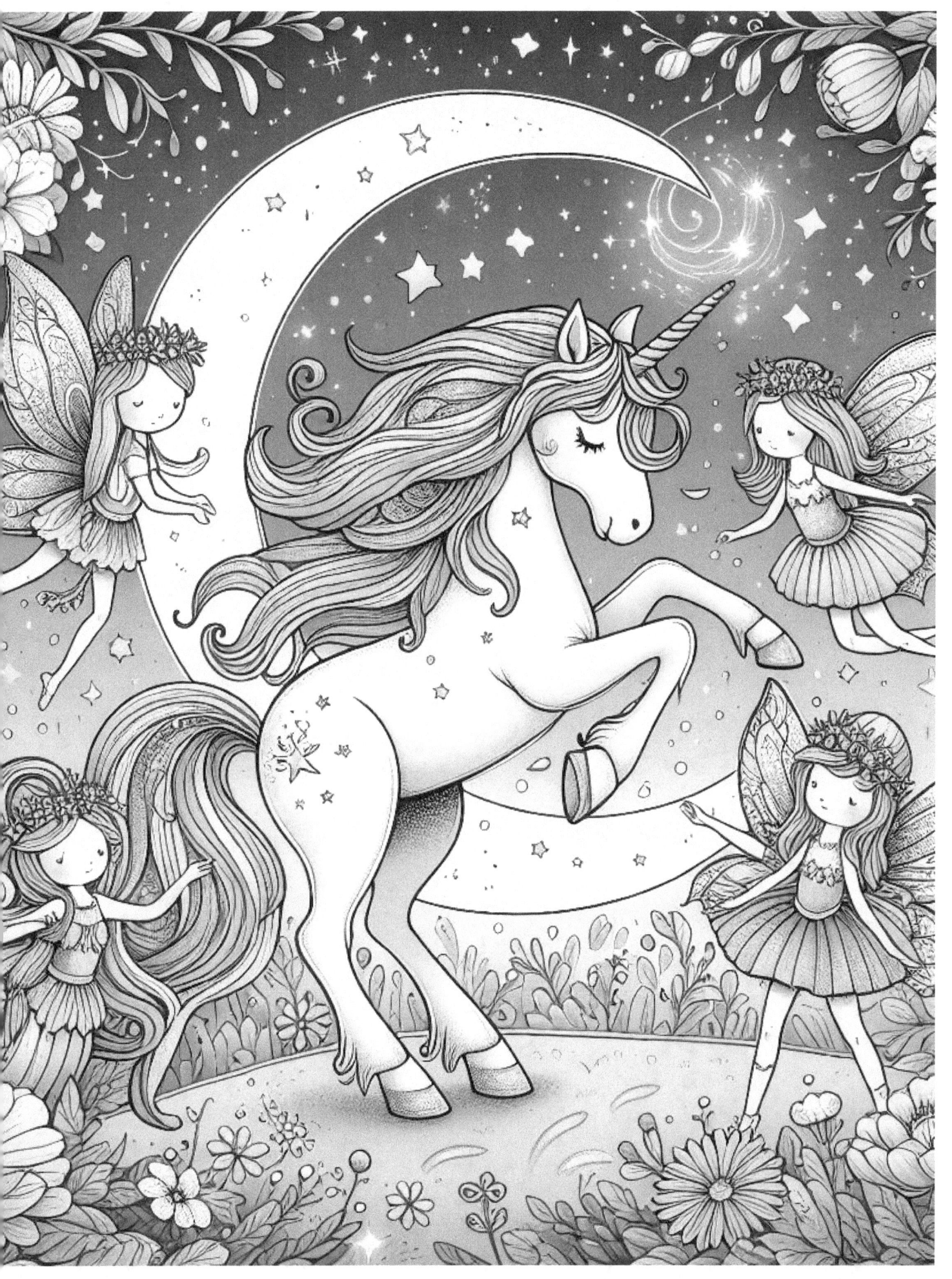

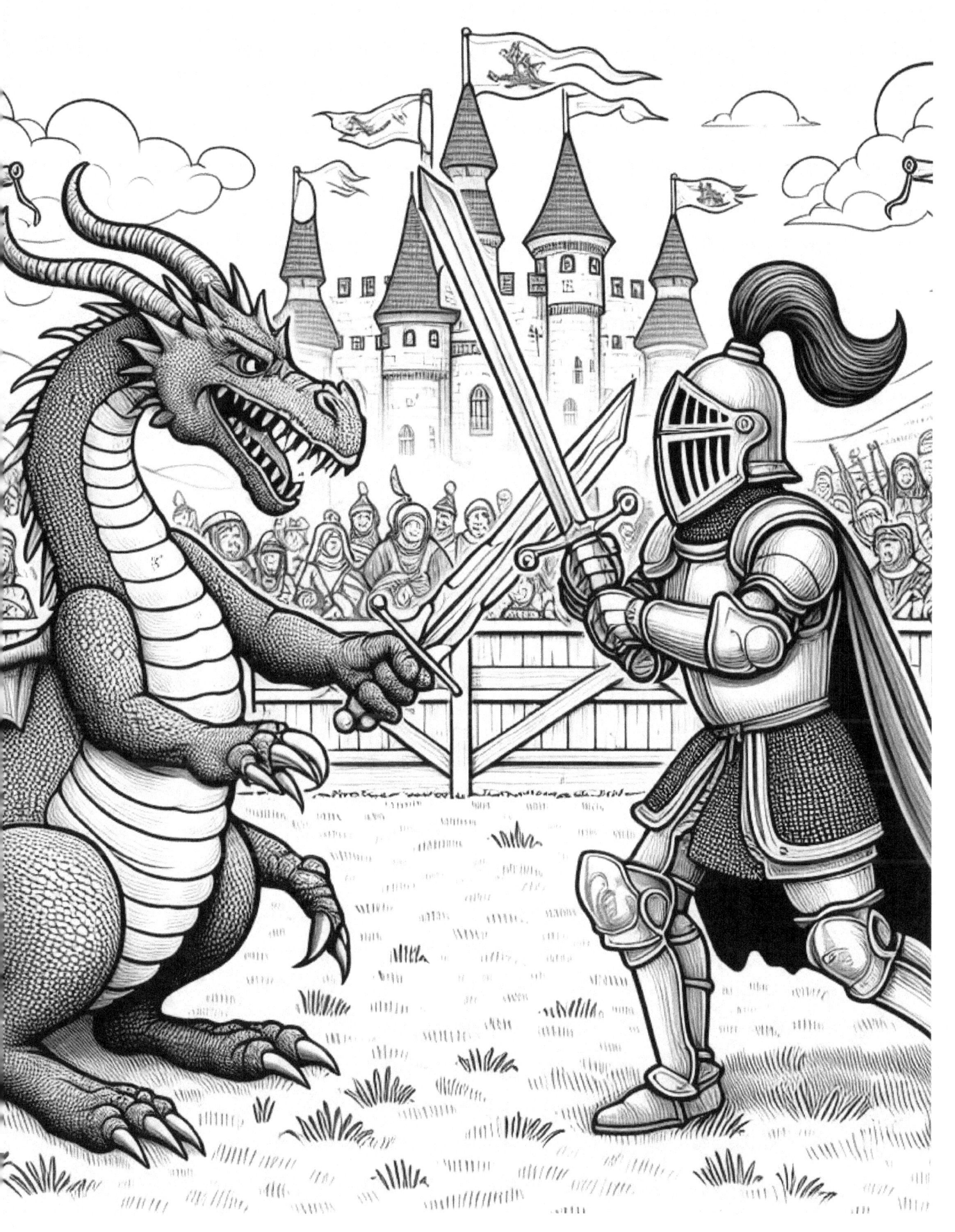

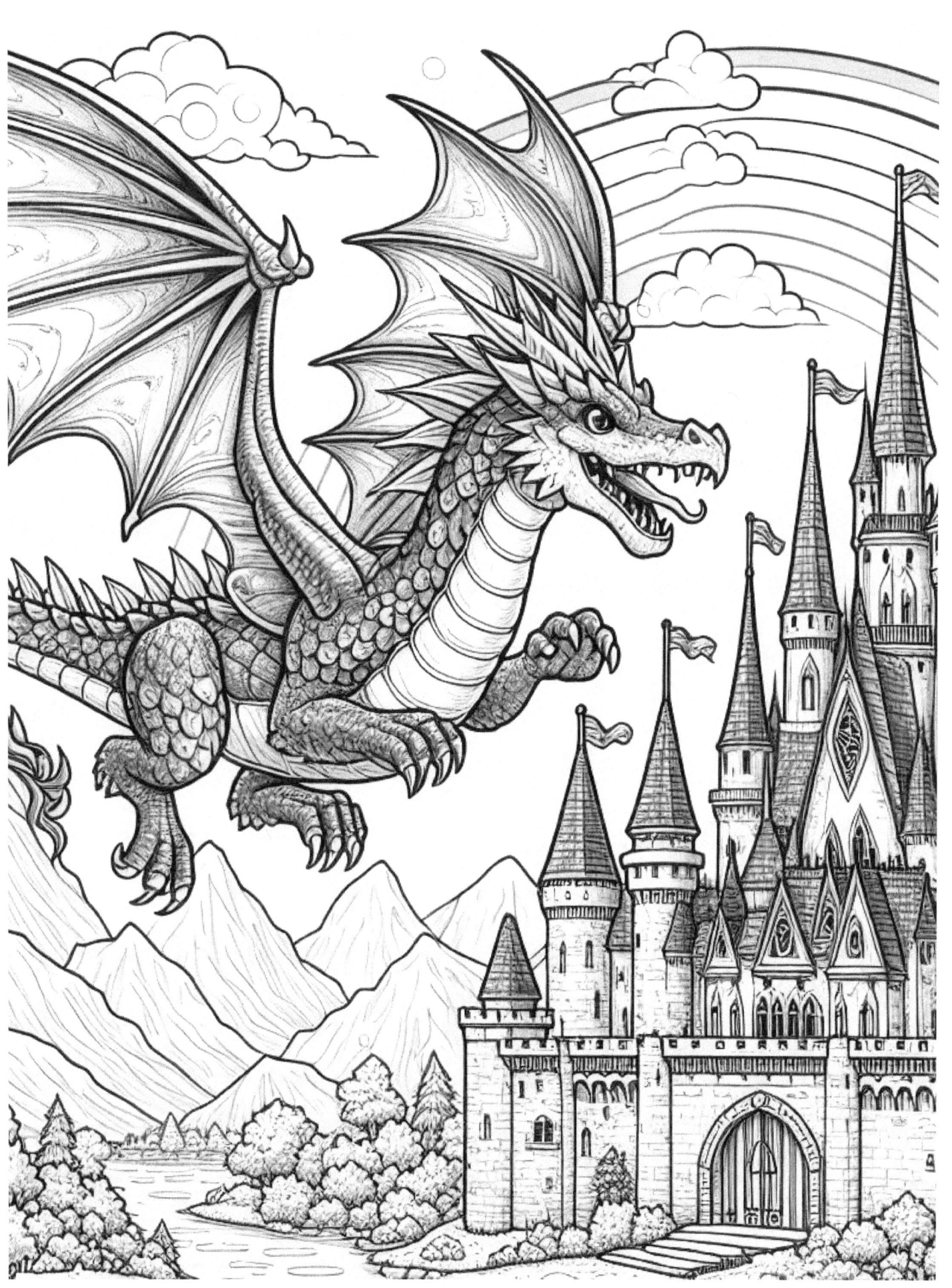

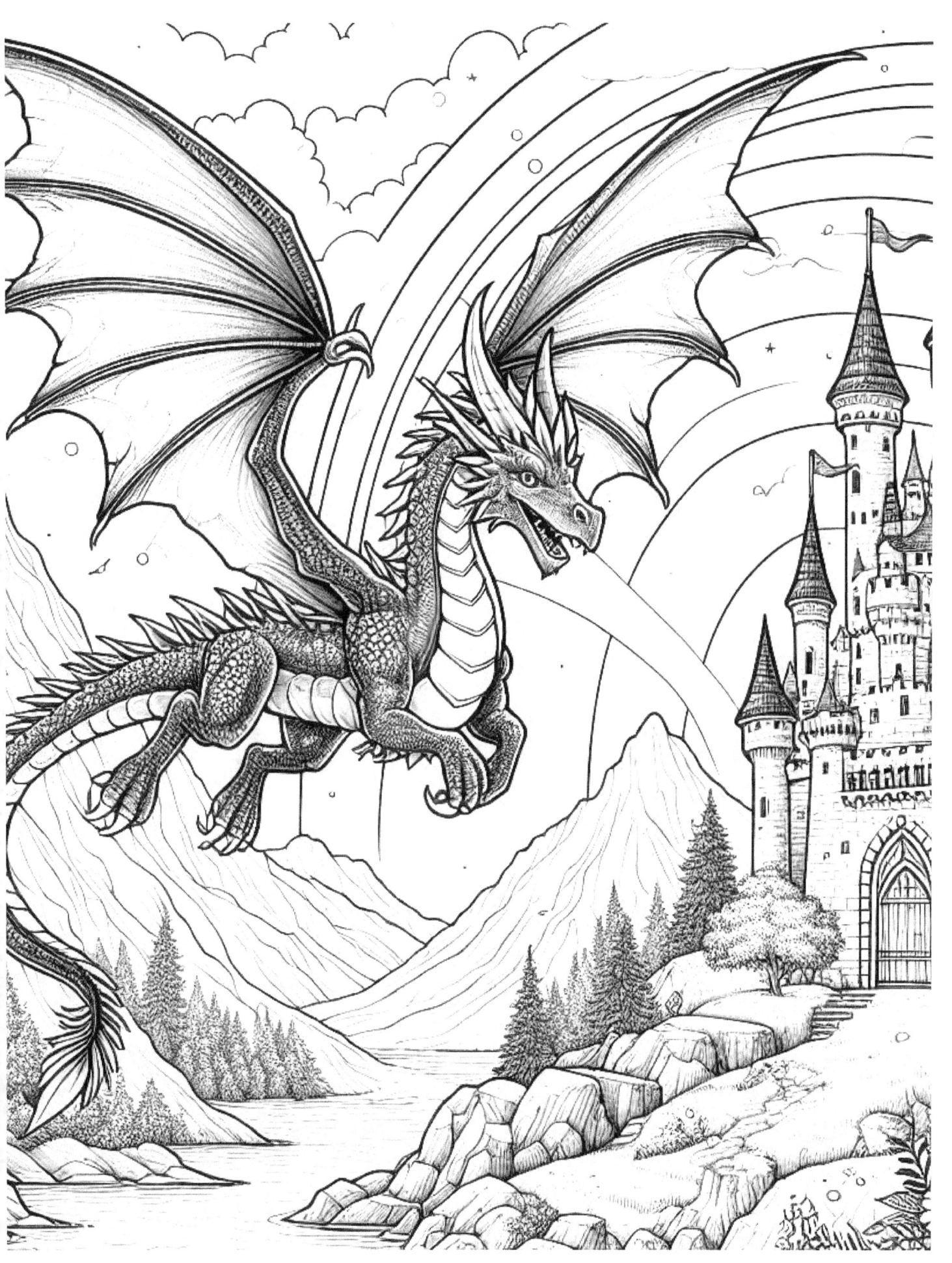

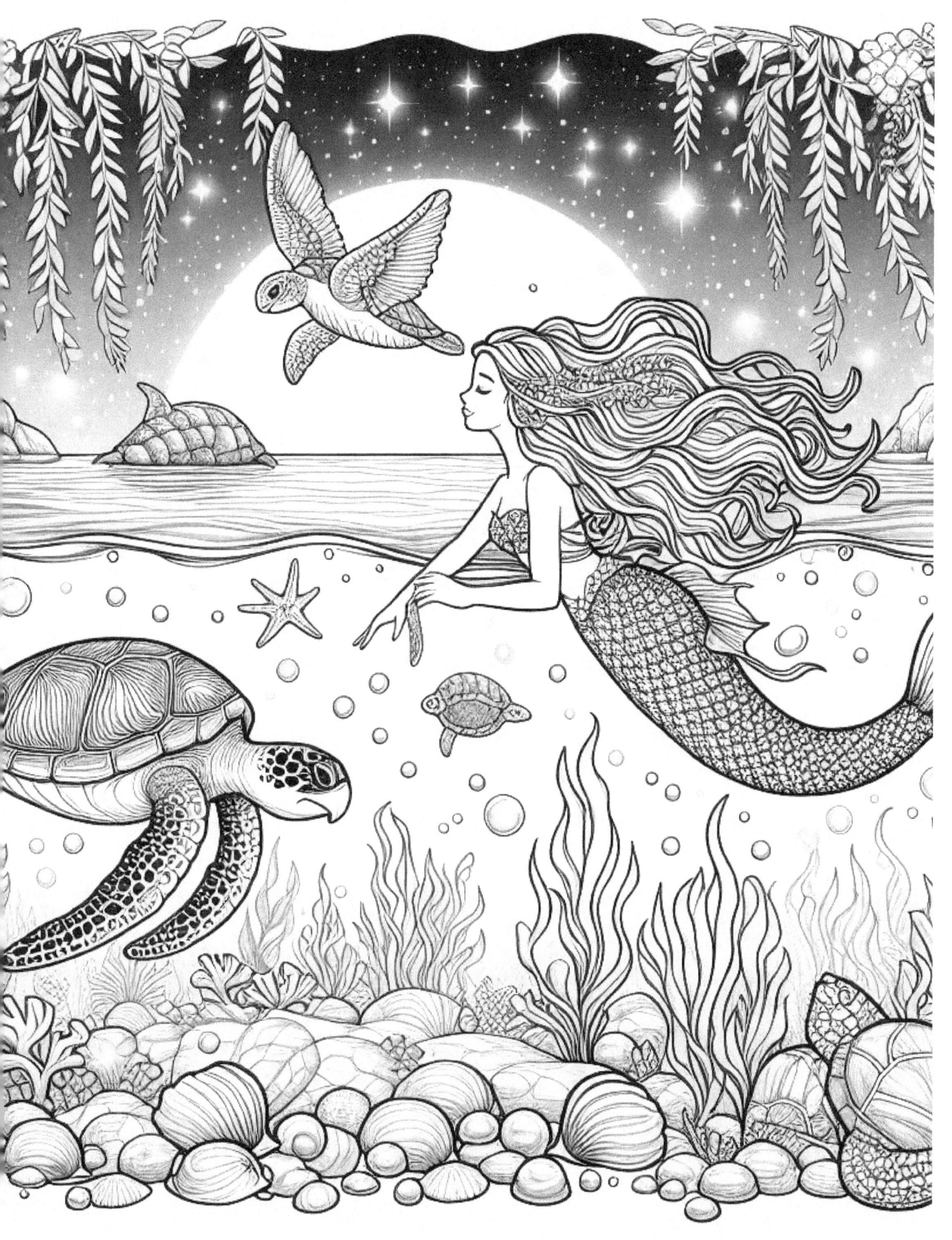

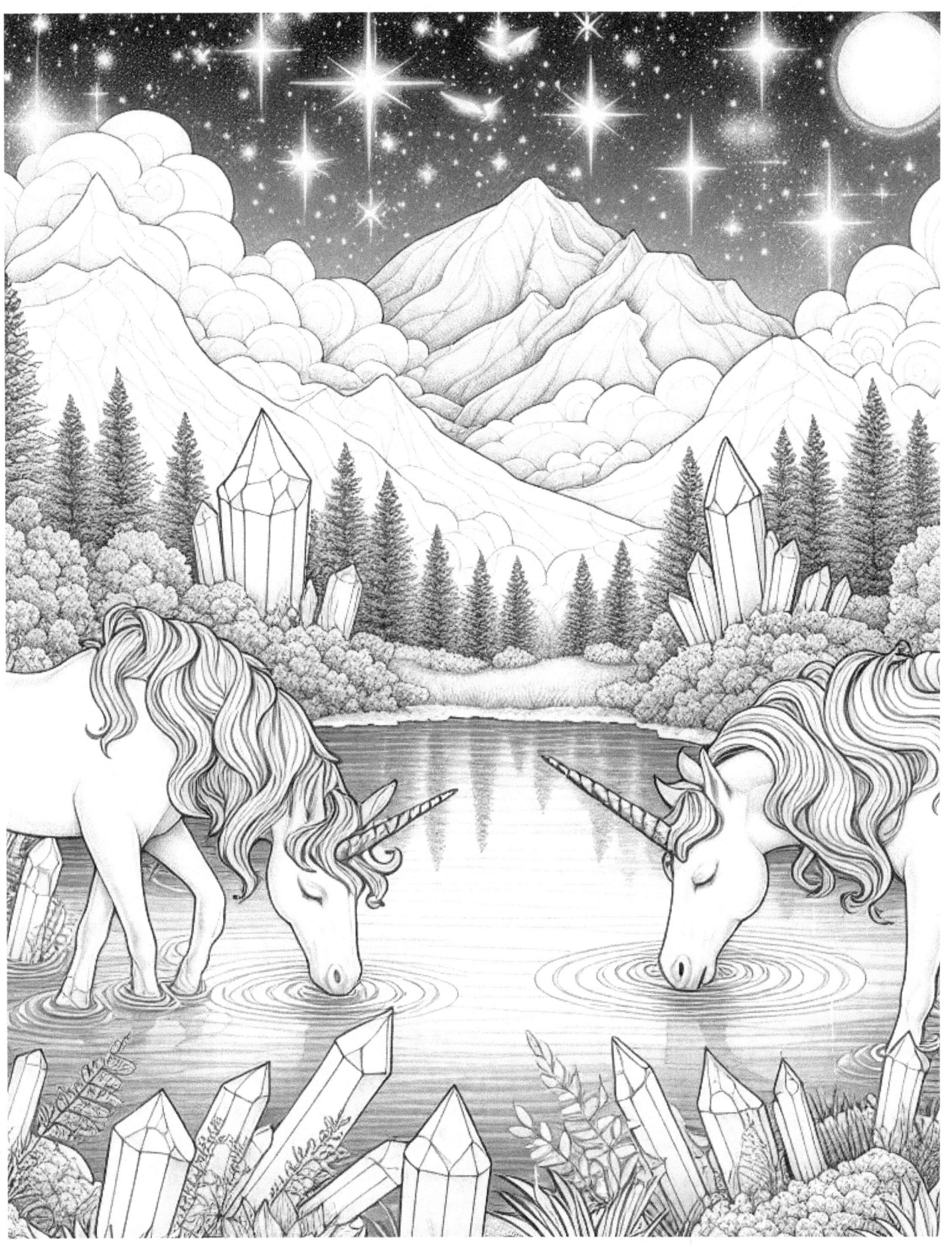

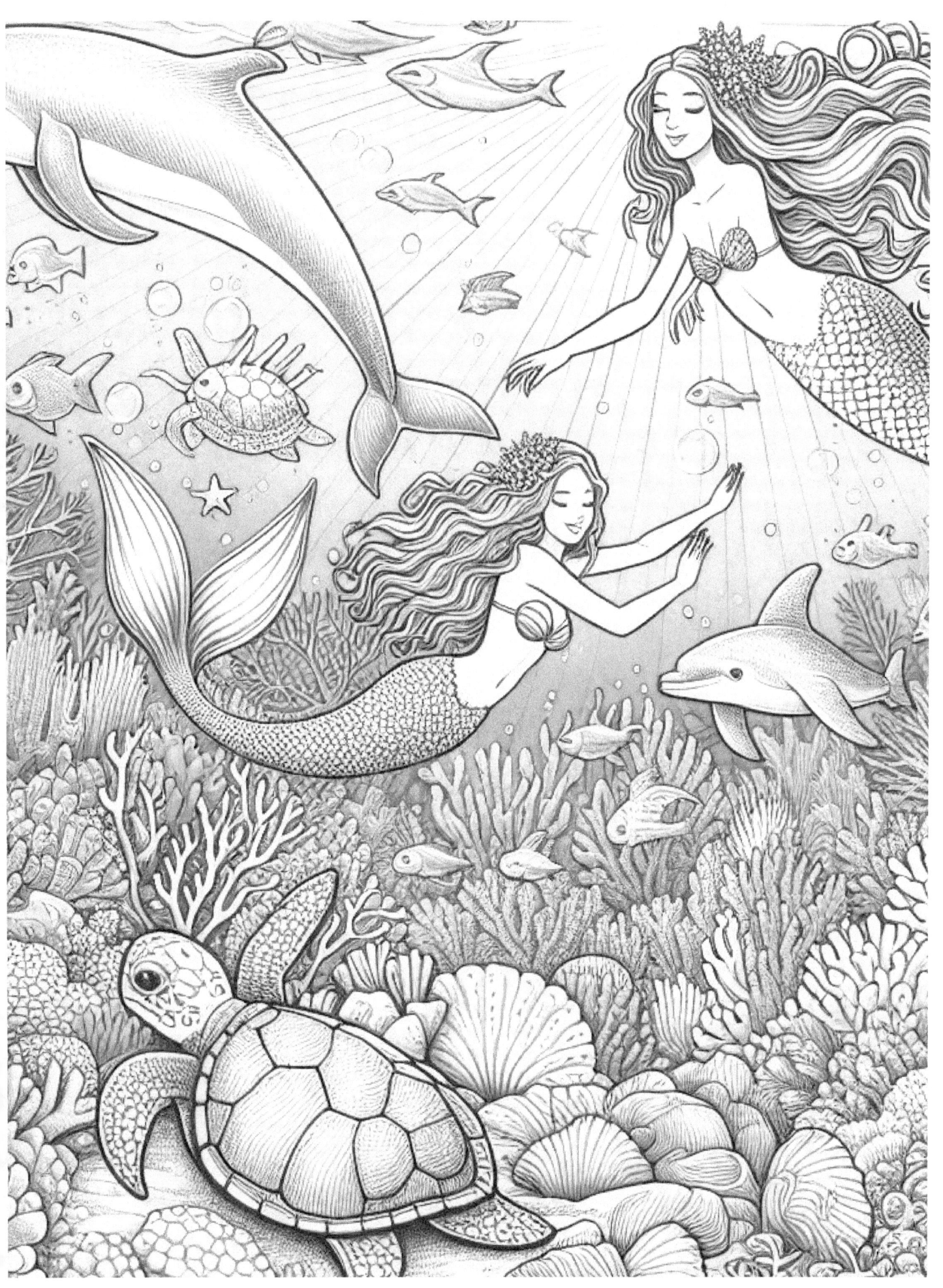

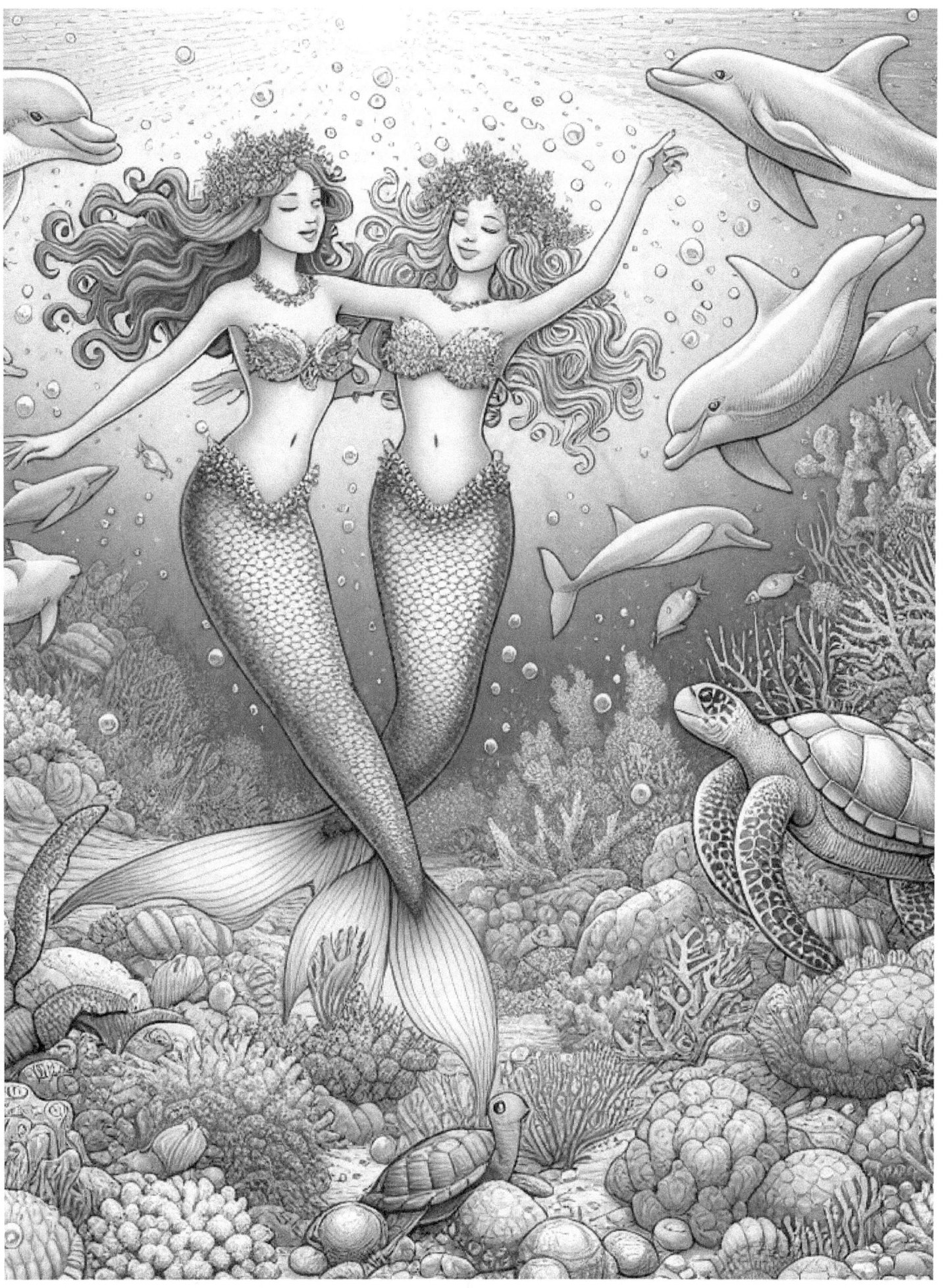

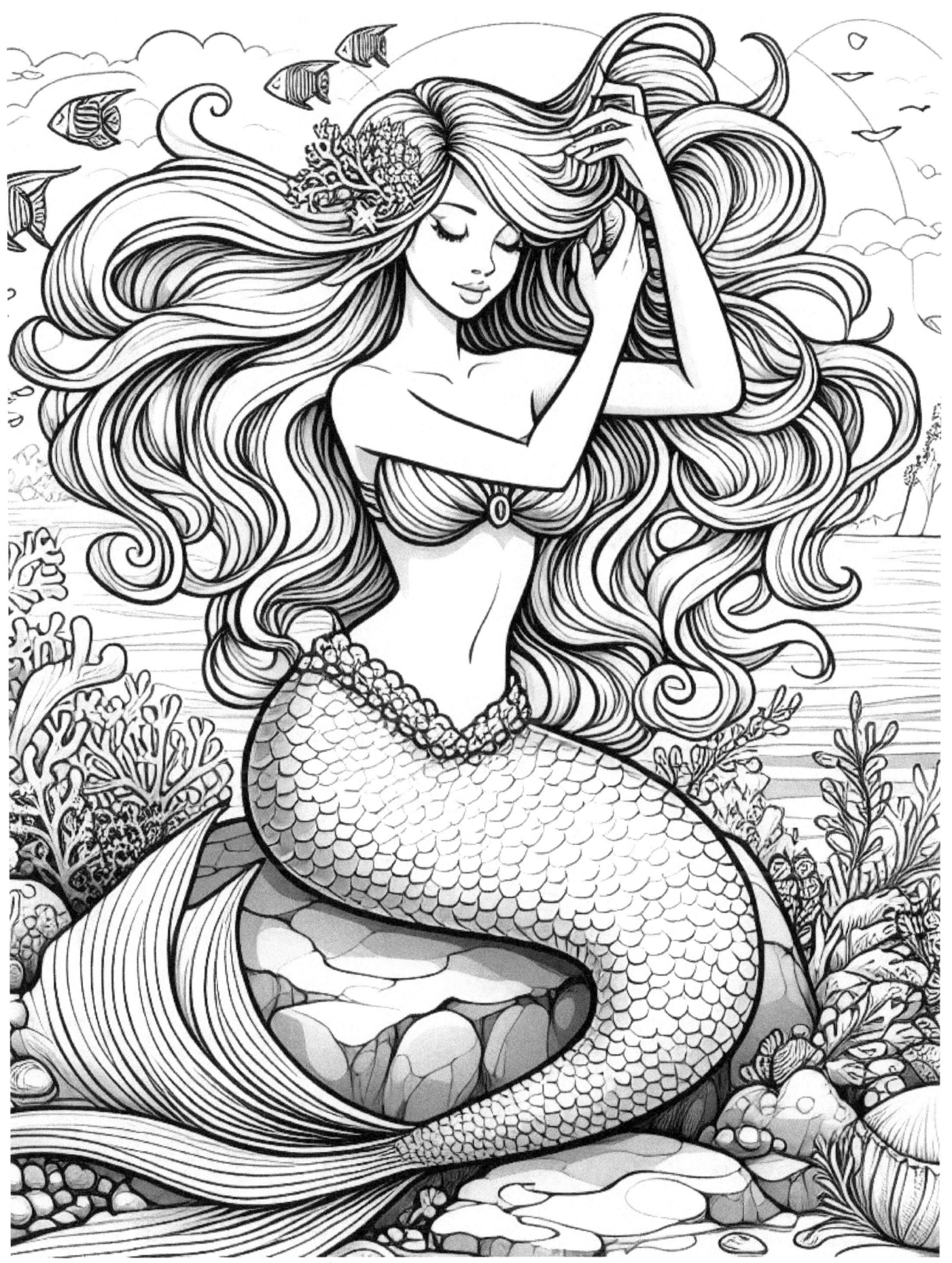

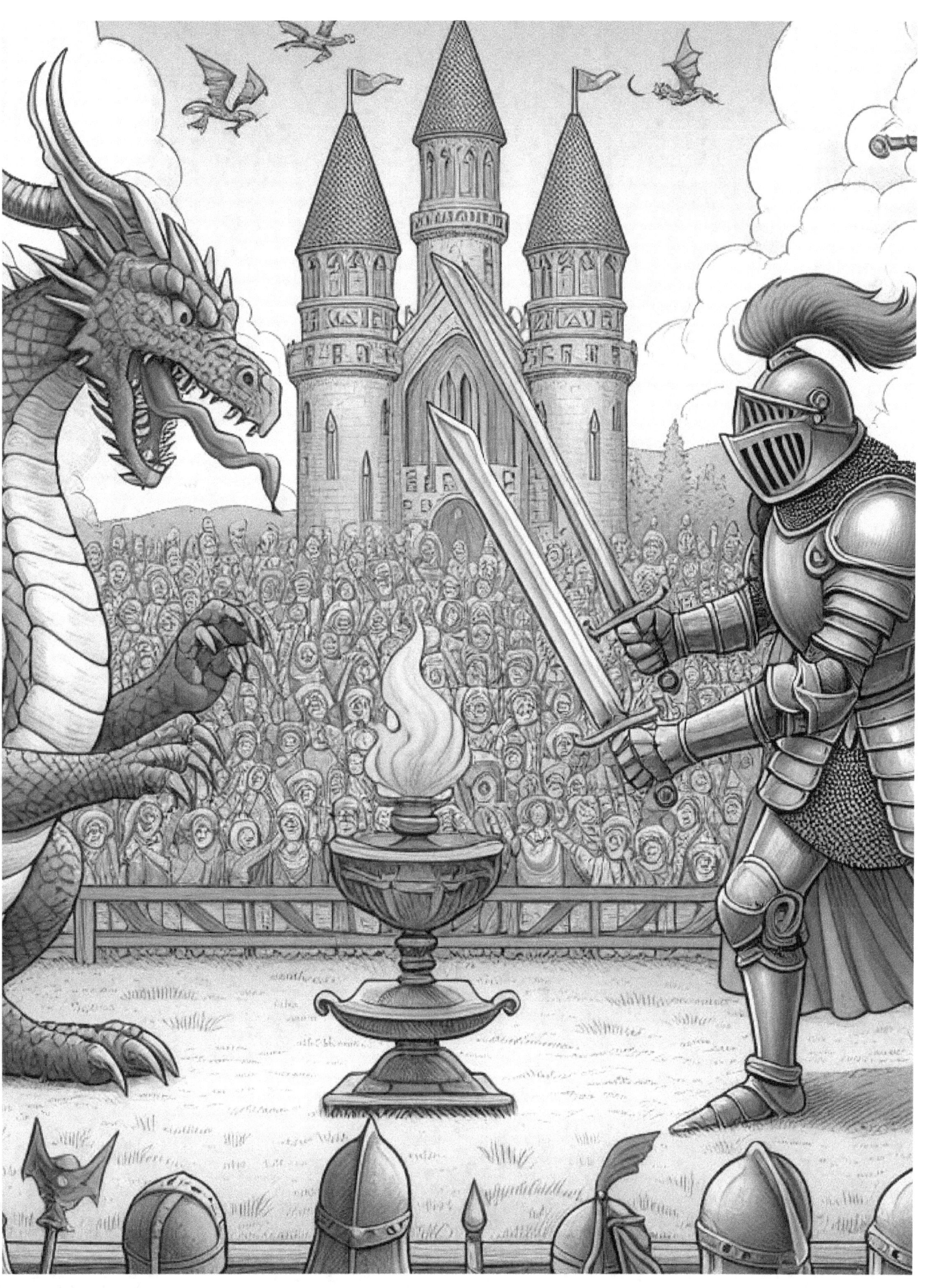

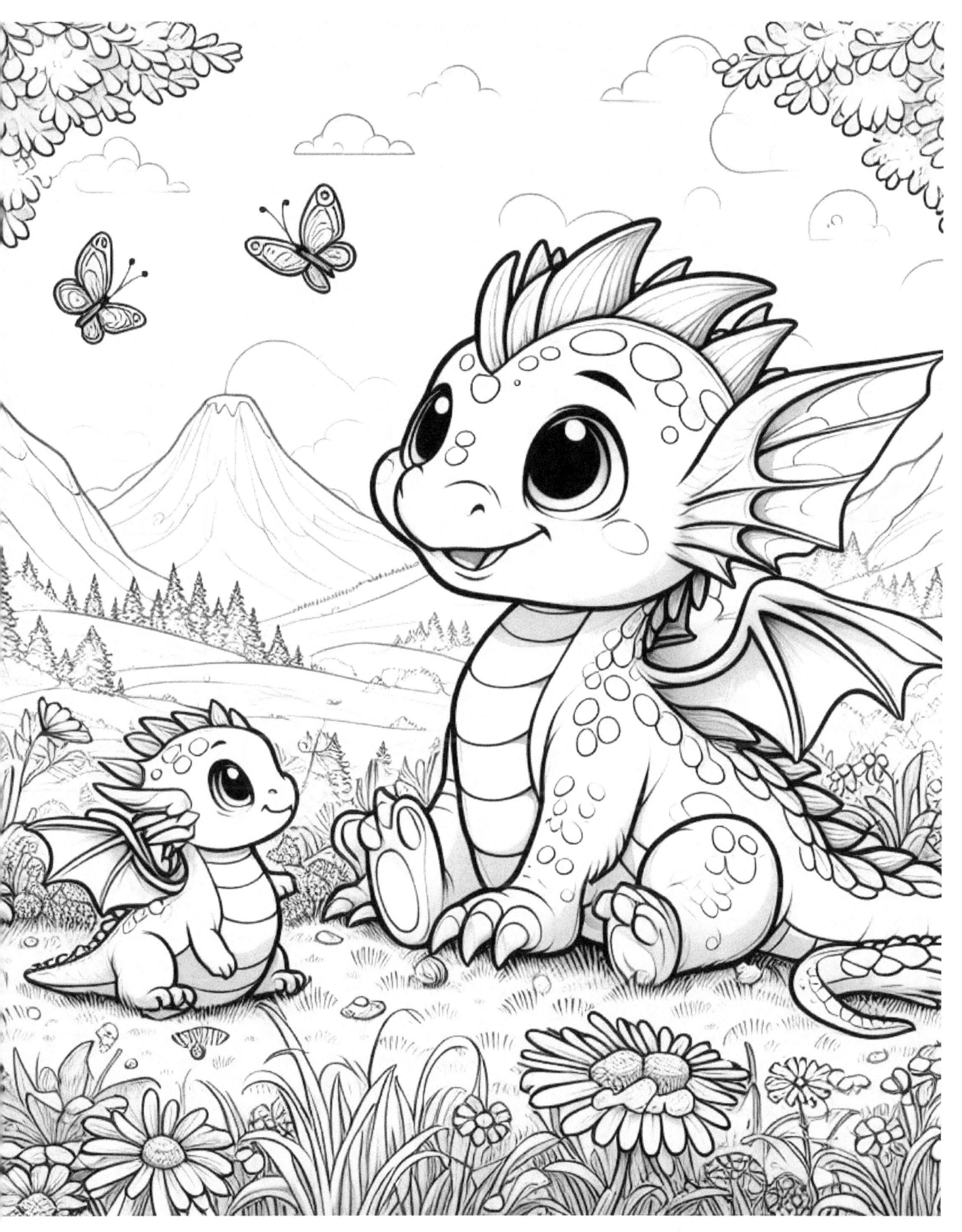

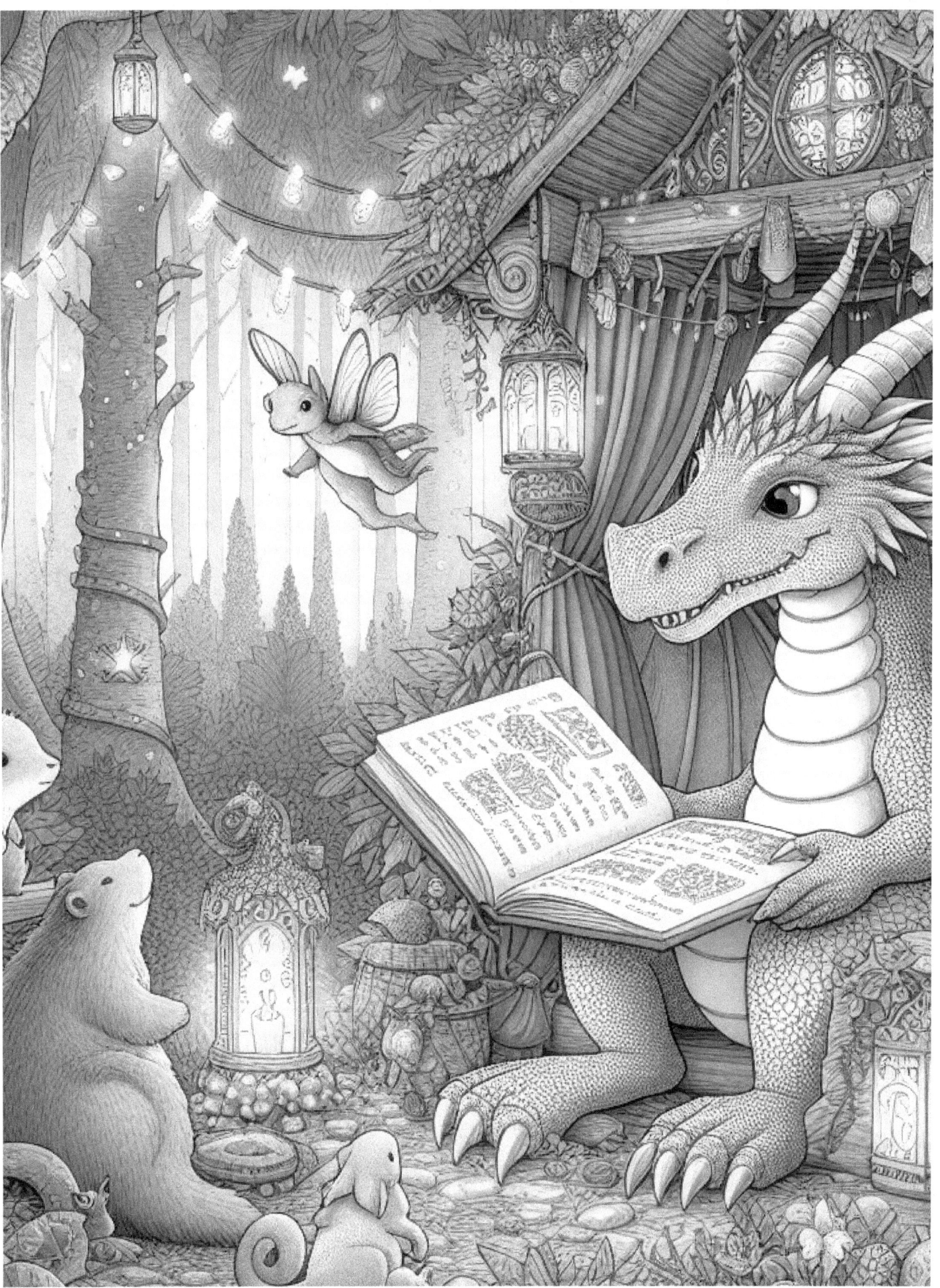

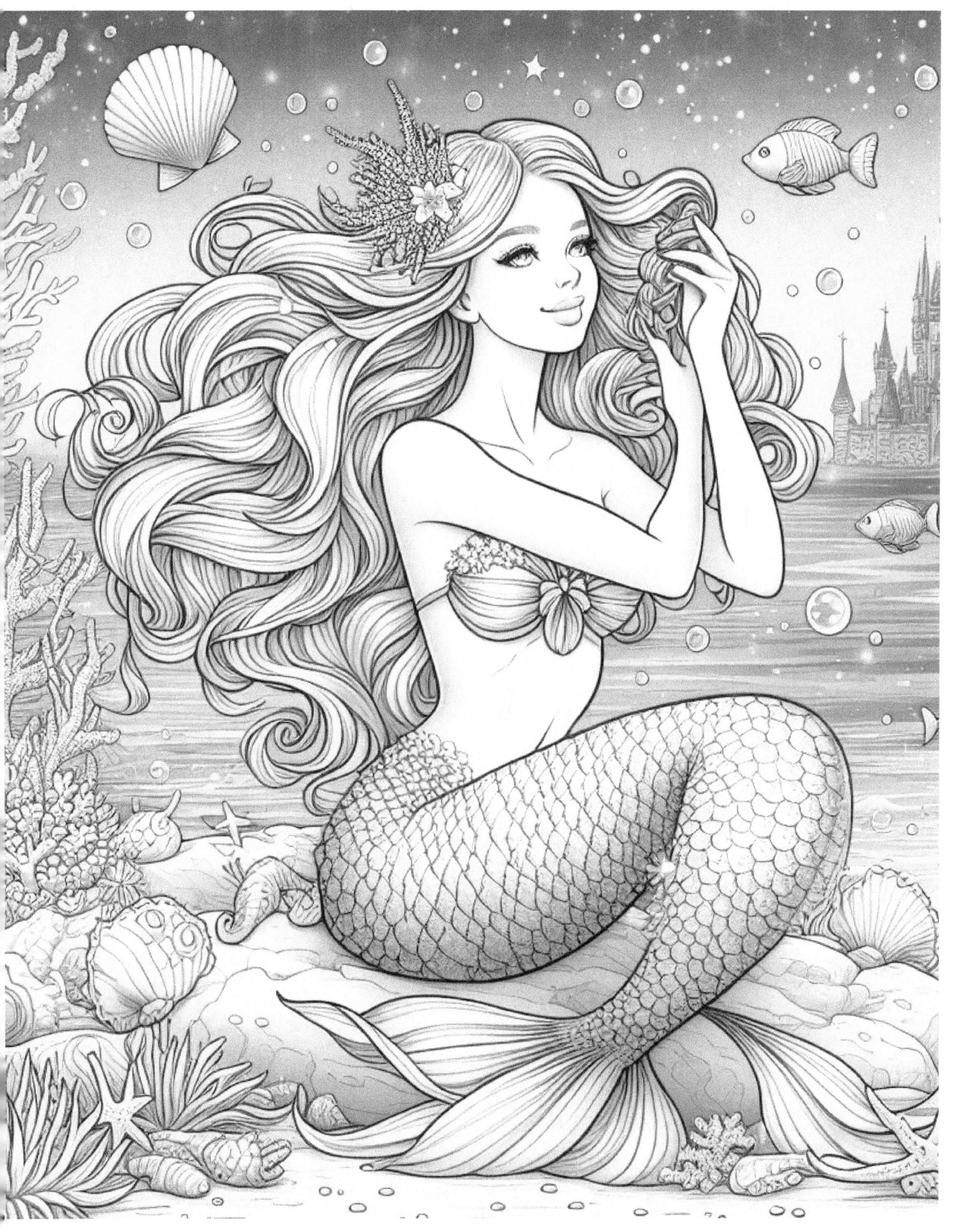

www.ingramcontent.com/pod-product-compliance
Lightning Source LLC
Chambersburg PA
CBHW082218220526
45470CB00010B/3221